SANDY

NEW YORK TIMES AND USA TODAY BESTSELLING AUTHOR
MELANIE MORELAND

Dear Reader,

Thank you for selecting the final book in the Vested Interest series. This has been a lovely journey for the past few years. I hope you've come to love these characters as much as I do.

Be sure to sign up for my newsletter for up to date information on new releases, exclusive content and sales.
Or visit https://www.subscribepage.com/melaniemoreland

Always fun - never spam!

xoxo,
Melanie

ALSO BY MELANIE MORELAND

SANDY by Melanie Moreland
Copyright © #1169995

ISBN Ebook 978-1-988610-35-1
Paperback 978-1-988610-34-4

MORELAND
BOOKS INC.

Edited by
Lisa Hollett—Silently Correcting Your Grammar

Cover design by Melissa Ringuette
Monark Design Services

DEDICATION

*Family is often not born of blood but
rather those special people who come into our lives and
become a part of our heart.*

*To those people in my life, thank you.
This one is for you.*

*And, as always,
for Matthew
who is my heart.*

ONE

SANDY

Thunder rolled, the intensity shaking the walls of my bedroom. Lightning followed, the room filling with vivid flashes of white, creating eerie shadows on the wall.

I shivered at the ferociousness of the storm and clutched my pillow tighter. I sighed as strong, warm arms slipped around me, and I was pulled into the loving embrace of my husband. His voice was low and comforting in the dark.

"It's all right, my girl. I have you."

I smiled at his endearment. I had been *his girl* from the day we met. Max was divorced, an established, well-respected physician, and twenty-two years my senior. His son, Aaron, was one of my best friends. Aaron and I enjoyed each other's company, but after one date, had agreed there was nothing between us and instead pursued an amazing friendship. He was close to his dad and talked about him often.

I saw them across the room at an event the university was hosting, and I went over to say hello to Aaron and meet his dad. The instant our eyes met, Max and I bonded. It was as if there was an invisible thread pulling us together, and neither of us could control the draw.

I never made it back to the dorm that night—Max and I were never apart again. We were married a short time later in a quiet ceremony and together weathered the stares, gossip, and slurs that followed us because of our age difference. Eventually, they died down, and we remained strong, proving them all wrong. Love wasn't about age. It was about your heart, the love it contained, and how you let that love guide you.

I relaxed into Max, allowing his strength to comfort me. "I hate storms," I murmured.

He kissed the sensitive spot behind my ear with a low chuckle. "I know. That's why I'm here."

"It's a bad one."

"It is," he agreed, his voice getting quieter. "But you're going to be fine. You're a strong, brave woman, Sandy. It's one of the reasons I loved you so much. You were my rock."

I frowned, a frightening grip forming in my chest. "Max, why do you sound so odd? Why are you talking in the past tense?"

"You know why. It's time, my girl. Time to move on."

A tremor went through me. "Max, no, please…"

I felt the light brush of his mouth on my shoulder. "You're fine, Sandy. I knew you would be. We both knew you would be. We wouldn't have been so solid together otherwise."

A tear ran down my cheek. "Stay, please."

"I can't, Sandy."

"Why?" I whimpered.

"Because I'm not really here. You need to find your happiness again." His voice drifted away. "You need that. I want that for you. But I love you, Sandy. I will always love you."

My eyes flew open. The storm was abating outside, the thunder a low boom in the distance.

I was curled in our bed, clutching Max's pillow, the blankets drawn tightly around me.

I was alone in the room, the bed feeling colder than usual. I sat up, flicking on the light and peering around the room.

I knew it was empty. I knew Max was gone. He'd never been here —it was simply another memory of the many times he'd held me during a storm.

He had passed over a year ago. Fifteen months, to be exact.

But there were moments, like this one, I swore he was close, even though I knew I had been dreaming.

It made my reality all that much lonelier.

Grief hit me, once again capturing me in its fist and squeezing hard.

I buried my face in my hands, and I wept.

TWO

SANDY

"Does anyone have anything to add?" Aiden asked, looking around the table. I glanced up from my pad of paper, pencil poised in readiness. Staff found it amusing I still took shorthand. Bentley found it invaluable. I was fast. I never missed a line at a meeting, and he found my notes helpful.

Everyone shook their head or remained silent. As usual, it had been a quick, informative meeting, each of the partners stating their thoughts or objectives, and giving enough information, there were few questions to be asked.

Exactly the way Bentley liked it.

He stood and clapped his hands, signaling the meeting was over. "All right. Have a productive day."

I jotted down the time and flipped the cover of my notepad closed. I began to stand, but Bentley held up his hand.

"A moment, Sandy."

He waited until everyone filed from the room, leaving only him, Aiden, Maddox, Reid, and me. Aiden shut the door and returned to the table.

For a moment, there was silence, all of the men glancing at one another, then at me, before their gazes skittered away. I frowned at the feeling of tension in the air and smoothed my hands over my skirt under the table, my palms suddenly damp.

Something was going on, and I didn't like it.

"Firing squad, boys?" I asked, trying to lighten the air.

Those words startled them, and they all began talking at once.

"Don't even joke about that, Sandy," Maddox muttered.

"Not in this lifetime," Aiden protested.

"I hardly think so," Bentley insisted.

Reid met my eyes, his gaze serious. A rare occurrence for Reid.

"We're worried about you, Sandy. We want to help."

His words stunned me into silence.

It was my job to worry about them, not the other way around.

"I'm fine," I protested. "Nothing to worry about."

Bentley cleared his throat. "Sandy—you forget how well we know you. You aren't fine, and we want to help."

"Am I not doing my job?" I retorted, not wanting to have this conversation with them. I knew it was born of concern and love, but I still wanted to avoid it.

"Of course you are. All of us, especially me, would be lost without you. You're the glue that holds this place together."

"Then perhaps a thank-you and not an inquisition would be more appropriate."

Bentley's shoulders stiffened, and his eyes narrowed.

"Give us the room," he said, his tone brooking no argument.

A moment later, we were alone. He leaned closer, pulling my notepad from my hands. "Talk to me, Sandy."

It was impossible to ignore the worry in his blue eyes. I sighed, the sound filled with sorrow.

"Sorry, Bentley. You hit me on a bad day."

"We're worried, Sandy. All of us. We want to help, but we don't know what to do. Tell me what you need." He wrapped his hands around mine, the stiff businessman disappearing and the warm, caring man I knew he kept hidden under his persona emerging. "We all love you, and we want to do something. Anything."

I smiled at him, shaking my head. "It's called grief, Bentley. There is nothing that you can do—that any of you can do. It's been well over a year, but at times it feels like yesterday. Other times, I cope well. I just have to handle each day as it comes." I huffed out a frustrated breath. "I didn't realize anyone noticed. I thought I was doing my job well."

"You are. But you forget how well we know you, Sandy. Your spark is missing. Your smile is forced. We all know how much you miss Max, and we want to do something. Anything. You just have to tell us what."

"Bring him back."

Bentley looked stunned at my words. "I can't do that," he said slowly.

I cupped his cheek. "Exactly. Bentley, no one can help. I have to get through each day the best way I can. Work helps—here, I'm busy and productive. Being part of your lives—seeing you all fall in love, start families, and be happy helps. I just need to do this in my own time. There's no manual when it comes to grief. No magic wand."

He dragged a hand through his hair. "That's what Emmy said. She told me to leave it alone. To let you grieve the way you need to grieve and just be there when you asked."

I smiled. "Emmy is a smart woman."

"But will you, Sandy? Will you come to us if we can help?"

His earnest sincerity rang out, and it made me smile. To the world, Bentley was rigid, stern, and unflappable. Underneath, he was caring, sweet, and always looking out for those he loved.

I was one of the lucky few that fell into that category.

"Yes, Bentley, if I need help, I will ask." I paused. "There is one thing."

"Anything."

"You and Emmy go out and let me have Addi for the night. I love spending time with that little one."

A grin pulled on his lips, softening his stern expression. His wife and daughter were the biggest chinks in his armor, and he adored them both.

"I think that helps me as much as it helps you," he stated dryly.

I shrugged. "But I'd like it."

"Then I'll arrange it."

"Are we done?"

He bent close, his voice serious. "We're here, Sandy. You are family —we all love you. Remember that, and all you have to do is ask. We'll be there. All right?"

6

My throat was thick.

I could only nod.

The rest of the day went quickly. Each of my boys stopped by my desk for a hug, a quiet word, or in Reid's case, a long visit. He pulled up a chair behind my "throne," as he called it, opened his laptop, and began to work.

"Problem with your office?" I asked, already knowing why he was there.

"Nope. I just like the view here better. I get to see you."

I squeezed his hand and let him stay. I adored the youngest member of the BAM family. A lost soul, he needed this place as much as it needed him. His upbringing had been horrendous, and there was something in his expression the day I met him that drew me to him. He lit my maternal instinct ablaze, and it had been I who insisted Aiden give him a chance. The more I got to know Reid, the more he pulled at my heartstrings. I loved all my boys, but Reid was special. Everyone knew it. But they felt much the same toward him. He was the boys' younger brother, and they looked out for him. We all did. In return, we had his fierce loyalty and affection.

We worked in companionable silence, broken only by the occasional call. My duties had changed when Max got sick. All the day-to-day business like answering the phone, or dealing with mail, and other smaller tasks went to a junior person in the office, but I handled everything that had to do with the partners. That alone kept me very busy.

Becca, Reid's live-in girlfriend, dropped by the desk. His smile for her was wide, his gaze filled with adoration as he looked at her. "Hey, B. Looking for me?"

She shook her head, ignoring his pout. "I'm looking for Sandy."

"What can I do for you?" I asked with a fond smile. She was good for Reid, and I liked her a lot. She was strong, capable, and completely infatuated with him. They were a great couple and spent a lot of time with me.

"Are you busy on Saturday?"

"No."

"Great. We're calling girls' time, and Emmy has booked a suite at The Four Seasons. Spa day!" She grinned.

"I see," I murmured, wondering how much this had to do with the conversation I'd had earlier with Bentley. It wouldn't surprise me that he asked Emmy to do something to cheer me up. Yet the thought of spending time with all the girls pleased me. And it would be a break from the constant quietness of the house.

"That sounds wonderful," I told her.

She beamed, her relief evident.

"Awesome. We'll go from here. Emmy has it all arranged. A driver, lunch, spa treatments, and pampering. Then to their place for dinner and movies afterward. He's having the meal catered."

"Wonderful. Thank you for including me."

She waved her hand. "Of course. You're one of us!"

She walked away, blowing Reid a kiss over her shoulder. He leaned close. "They want you there, you know."

"I know," I agreed. "It's a lovely thought."

He chuckled. "I made sure to add some of your favorite red wine to the menu."

"Does Bentley know you did that?" I asked, one eyebrow raised in question, my theory now confirmed.

He grinned. "I helped choose the menu. We got everyone's favorites. We're gonna have a guys' day at Bentley's while you girls are busy. Well, us, and Addi."

I laughed. Addi was doted on by all her uncles. She was a lucky little girl.

"I don't think Addi is quite ready for pizza and wings."

He winked. "We got chicken fingers and fries for her. Shake up that 'bottle only' diet thing she's got going. Give her something new to try. I ordered the dipping sauce mild."

I laughed at his silly comments. "Good luck with that."

He became serious. "I want you to have a good time. Relax. Enjoy yourself."

I stood and bent low, kissing his cheek. "I'll try."

"Please have a good time," he whispered. "Max would want you to laugh and enjoy yourself."

I nodded, unable to speak. He was right. Max and I had talked about his death a lot when we were first together. Given our age difference, it seemed a natural conclusion, one day I would be without him. But back then, it seemed far away and remote. It was easy to laugh and tease. To tell him I would get a younger man next time around. A boy toy.

"We'll spend all your money on sex and booze," I swore.

Max had laughed when I made that statement.

"You do that, my girl. Someone who loves an older, sexy woman. Make sure he treats you right while he's spending my money. Make him earn it."

I winked at him. "I'll do that."

Once he was diagnosed with late-onset MS, the conversations were numerous but not as funny. Even then, I was in denial he would ever leave me. I couldn't imagine life without him.

Now, I was having trouble remembering life with him. Happiness seemed difficult to find and harder to hold.

Life was harder.

I cupped Reid's cheek and offered him a tight smile.

"I'll do my best."

The suite rang with laughter. There were three different treatment areas set up, and I had taken advantage of them all. My skin was glowing, my nails buffed, and my toes sparkled with fresh polish. I sighed as I rolled my shoulders, the massage having worked wonders on my sore muscles. Max always teased me that I carried my tension in my shoulders. *"Like cement,"* he would mumble while trying ineffectually to rub them. While his embraces and soft words were perfection, his massage technique was terrible. After a few bumbling, inept attempts on his behalf to rub my shoulders early on in our relationship, he treated me to a bimonthly massage. After he died, I had stopped going. I stopped doing a lot of things.

I looked around the room, smiling at the girls. Young, happy, and in love, they all made me smile, even as my heart ached to remember that time in my life. I loved that they included me in their girl time. To me, they were all extensions of my family—adopted daughters—and I loved them all.

Becca came out of the bathroom, wrapped in a thick, white terry cloth robe. Her skin glowed—from the facial or the wine she had consumed I wasn't sure, but she looked radiant. She had been late this morning, blushing as she rushed out to the car, Reid following her and catching her before she stepped in to kiss her long and lovingly. Judging from the smug expression on his face, there was no doubt as to why we waited for her, and it had set the tone for the day with constant teasing and banter.

She flung herself beside me with a grin. *"How you doin'?"* she winked and deadpanned. "Looking good, Sandy."

I laughed. "So do you."

Her phone buzzed and I chuckled. "I think Reid is missing you today."

She rolled her eyes, but her grin was wide. "I think he is. My phone has been blowing up all day."

I patted her hand. "That's a good thing, Becca. Enjoy it."

She nodded, her eyes on the screen. "I do. I love his silly texts and pictures."

"He worships you," I informed her.

Her cheeks flushed, and this time, I knew it wasn't the wine. "The feeling is mutual."

"I know."

Cami and Dee strolled over to the seating area and curled up on the sofa across from us. Like me, they were both relaxed from their pampering. Liv and Emmy were finishing up with their massages and would join us. Bentley had arranged not only a light lunch, but a full afternoon tea to be served in the room. He knew how much I enjoyed a real afternoon tea, and I was touched by his efforts.

We chatted and laughed until the rest of the girls joined us. We sat, sipping our beverages and talking about a multitude of things. Life, houses, work, motherhood, and finally, the conversation turned to men. There was some oversharing, funny stories, and cute moments of the antics of all their men, and Becca turned to me.

"Sandy," she began.

I shook my head. "I know what you're about to say, Becca. I'm fine. Honestly, I am. I have bad days, and one in particular last week, but that is to be expected."

Emmy leaned forward, taking my hand. "What brought it on, Sandy?"

With a sigh, I told them about the storm and my dream. They all had tears in their eyes as I recalled Max's words.

"Do you think it was real?" Dee asked quietly. "Do you think Max was telling you it's time to move on?"

I shrugged, unsure how to answer. It had felt real. His words had echoed the sentiments he had expressed so often when we would discuss the future and he would insist I had to accept the thought of one without him. How he wanted me to find happiness and love again.

"You have too much in you to give to spend the rest of your life grieving for me, my girl."

"I can't fathom loving anyone else, Max," I informed him. It was the simple truth.

He had run his fingers over my cheek. "Not the way you love me, but you can love again, Sandy. I want you to. I need to know you will be happy again once I am gone."

I had promised him I would try, but the truth was, I had no idea how to do so or if I even had it in me to attempt it.

I said so to the girls.

"Colin lectures me all the time to go out and start living again."

Becca interrupted me. "I still can't believe that fine specimen is your *grandson*. You're too young to have him be your grandkid."

I chuckled. "*Fine specimen.* I'll keep that one to myself. But I'll take the compliment. One of the perks of marrying an older man, I suppose." I sighed. "Colin insists it's time for me to move forward, and he hates to see me wasting away, as he calls it. Aaron agrees with him. He tells me his father would want me to be happy," I admitted.

"What do you think?" Emmy asked, still holding my hands.

"I don't know how to move forward," I stated. "I have no idea how to meet someone or start again. Things have changed since I dated thirty-some-odd years ago. I don't think people meet at clubs or dances now."

All the girls laughed.

"No," Becca agreed. "It's online most of the time."

I nodded in resignation. "Colin said the same thing. He says it easier to meet women that way. Seems so impersonal to me."

The girls laughed.

"Trust me, sometimes there is *too* much personal." Cami smirked.

I chuckled. "In my day, you went out. Locked gazes with someone. Talked. Felt that connection. How can you do that with a computer screen?"

Emmy agreed. "I—we—all got lucky we met the men we did and the way we did."

Cami nodded. "Yes—I tried my share of dating apps. Thank goodness those days are behind me."

I pursed my lips. "Colin told me he had a date at Tinder last week. He has mentioned that place a couple of times since his girlfriend dumped him. I assumed Tinder was a restaurant he was meeting them at. I suppose I assumed wrong?"

The girls dissolved into laughter. Becca wiped her eyes. "You did. Tinder isn't a restaurant."

"It's one of these dating apps?"

"Well, it's not for, ah, *dating*, Sandy. It's more for, um, hookups," she explained, trying to hide her amusement.

"Hookups," I repeated slowly. I widened my eyes in shock.

"*Hookups?* Are you telling me Colin is having casual sex with strange women?"

"Quite possibly." Emmy smirked. "Not sure how casual, of course."

"Well, that little...*scamp.*" I shook my head. "I hope he's being safe. I'll have to ask him. Or perhaps I'll save us both the embarrassment and simply buy him a box of condoms as a reminder."

This caused more laughter.

"I'm not particularly interested in sex with a stranger, girls."

"We know that," Emmy assured me. "But maybe just meeting some nice men? At least trying?"

Becca leaned forward, earnest. "Even if you find someone to be friends with. Go out to dinner with—or a movie. You always loved to dance. Wouldn't it be nice to go with someone? That wouldn't be so bad, would it?"

I mulled over her words. "No, I suppose it wouldn't. But I have no idea how to do that dating app thing."

Liv pulled her laptop from her bag and handed it to Becca. "But we do."

I sighed as I watched Becca's fingers fly over the keys. I wondered what I had just gotten myself in to.

And I knew, without a doubt, this had been their plan all along.

———

Dinner at Bentley's was, as usual, wonderful. I was able to spend time with Addi, feeding her, having cuddles, her little body warm and soft in my arms. I left not long after dinner, insisting I was too tired for their movie marathon. Frank, Bentley's driver, took me home—all the boys had been drinking, so Bentley had him on standby to take everyone home safely. There were hugs and kisses all around when I left. The girls never mentioned the dating app, for which I was grateful. I wasn't sure how the boys would react to the news, and I hadn't yet decided to go ahead with the idea.

Late Sunday afternoon, I sat in front of my laptop, looking over the profile Becca had created for me. She insisted she had done thorough research on the various "apps," as she called them, and that Mature Matchups had a good reputation, didn't promote promiscuity, and many of the profiles on the site were people like me—looking for someone to socialize with, a friend to have dinner, see a movie, "hang out," as she called it.

"No hookups?" I asked, straight-faced.

She bit her lip. "Um..."

I patted her hand with a grin. "Teasing."

"If romance enters the picture, then it does," she assured me. "If not, having a friend to go out with isn't a bad thing, is it?"

I had to admit she was right. When Max became ill, our social life had changed—not that it was ever the same as other couples. We were very close and enjoyed each other's company. With the huge age difference between us, we were mostly shunned when we were first married so we had relied on each other for everything. Max was my best friend, shopping partner, confidant, and lover—all rolled into one. Over the years, we made some couple friends, but with his busy career and schedule, those times were limited. I was fine with it—I had been a bit of a loner, preferring reading and taking courses over other, more social activities. My husband and grandkids—especially Colin—kept me busy, and my life, once I met the BAM boys and Bentley opened his company, had revolved around them. Now, my nights and weekends once spent with Max, were long and empty at times.

Perhaps a friend wouldn't be such a bad thing. If I went into this idea seeking companionship instead of a romantic interest, I might find someone whose company I would enjoy. Someone who could help make me feel a little less lonely.

I scanned the profile once again. It was exactly as Becca promised. A simple picture, a brief bio, and the language was correct. Nothing suggesting anything except looking to meet someone my age with similar interests to be friends. It was perfect.

Yet, I couldn't bring myself to press the "activate" button on the screen.

I shook my head. I was being silly. Nothing ventured, nothing gained. And the girls had gone to so much effort and assured me unless I gave out the information, the profile was private, and I could delete it at any time. Before I could change my mind, I clicked the button, then shut the lid and hurried away from my desk as if the machine itself were going to start spitting out names of "matches."

I went to the kitchen and poured a glass of wine.

As Aiden would often say—I was too old for this shit.

M onday morning, my phone buzzed with another incoming message.

"You have a match."

It had started about an hour after I clicked activate. I hadn't realized Becca had added the app to my phone as well. I had muted the sound, but it still vibrated every time, and even in the pocket of my suit jacket, it made itself known.

Once again, Bentley's gaze strayed to my phone as it signaled another message.

"Are you sure you don't have to get that, Sandy?" he asked, his brow furrowed.

I shook my head. It was rare my phone rang at work these days, but this morning, it was going off constantly.

"It's fine," I assured him. "I somehow got on a call list. I'll handle it when we're done."

Aiden spoke up. "I can take care of that for you, Sandy. Give me your phone, and I can get it to stop."

"No!" I exclaimed, my voice rising a little.

All three partners looked surprised at my reaction. Reid was late this morning, having an appointment outside of the office. I was glad of that fact since Reid knew me so well. Even though the girls had said they wouldn't say anything about the dating site, now that I had activated my profile, I knew it was going to come out eventually. I was in no hurry for the boys to know what I had done. I had a feeling none of them would approve, and I wasn't in the mood to handle their objections or worries. They were all very protective of me.

"It's fine," I insisted. "I'll handle it. Now, you were saying, Bentley?"

"Ah, yes." He frowned but let the subject drop. "I am going to see a couple of places this afternoon with Van that have come up unexpectedly. Can you clear my schedule?"

"Of course."

"Richard is flying in next week to firm up some new ideas for Phase Two of the towers," Maddox stated. "You'll need some extra bagels in the kitchen."

I smiled as I jotted down the reminder. Richard was one of my favorites, and I looked forward to his trips here. I had a feeling they were more frequent than needed since Becca was here every day, but he had a close bond with Maddox, and the partners respected him immensely and appreciated his personal touch on the account.

"On it. I'll get that vegetable cream cheese he is so fond of in as well."

"He gets all the good stuff," Aiden moaned.

I laughed, indicating the plate of Danishes on the boardroom table. "I don't think you go short, Aiden."

"We're your favorites, right?" he countered. "You love us best. Especially me."

"I don't think so," Maddox snorted. "Sandy digs my vibe. I'm her fave."

"I highly doubt it," Bentley interjected. "I found her. She was mine first, therefore it stands to reason she prefers me over you two clowns."

"You're all wrong. I'm her favorite," Reid announced as he strolled in. "Richard is second, and you three pull up the rear. Exactly where you should be."

"I don't think so," Aiden huffed. "She's been ours longer, so we rank higher. Right, Sandy?"

I stood, snapping closed my notepad. "A mother never has favorites." I winked. "At least, that is what we tell you all." But I patted Reid's cheek as I went by, making him grin.

Reid threw himself into a seat. "Told you."

Aiden cursed loudly. "I hired you. I can fire you too."

"Nope. Sandy won't let you. I'm her *favorite*." Reid plucked a Danish off the plate and took a big bite. "Besides, you love me too, you big lug."

"Not if you keep eating my Danishes."

"Will you two shut up?" Bentley groaned. "This is an office, not a playground."

But he winked at me as I left the office. I shut the door behind me with a smile. It didn't matter how old, rich, or successful they were, they would always be my boys.

They were *all* my favorites. I adored each one of them for their own special reason. They all needed me in some fashion, but Reid's need was the deepest of them all, and I had responded to that need the moment I met him. But they were all lights in my life.

My phone buzzed again, and I sighed.

Maybe that should be enough.

H ell broke loose about three o'clock. Reid rushed past my desk, casting a worried glance my way as he hurried by, disappearing into Aiden's office. With a frown, I asked the person I was speaking with on the phone to repeat themselves, only to be startled by the loud curse coming from Aiden's office. Seconds later, they both disappeared into Maddox's office. I shook my head, wondering what crisis was occurring now. Something big in IT land or a glitch in the security system Reid was diligently working on, adding upgrades or tweaking.

I had my answer soon enough when the three of them appeared in front of my desk. Their countenances were serious, and they looked upset.

A flicker of fear went through my chest.

"What is it?" I asked. "Bentley? Is he all right?" I had spoken with

17

him not long ago, and he said he was on his way back to the office. Had there been an accident?

Aiden shook his head. "Bent's fine. He'll be here in a moment. We need to talk to you."

I furrowed my brow. "Fine. About?" My gaze fell to Reid's hand. He was holding his phone, which was nothing new, but what was on the screen explained the intensity of their expressions and the tense set of their shoulders.

My profile on Mature Matchups was on his phone. And the protective, worried faces were exactly what I knew would happen if they discovered it.

"My personal life is not up for discussion," I stated mildly.

"Sandy." Aiden bent forward, his voice low. "These sites can be dangerous."

"Becca checked it out."

"Becca should have minded her own business," Reid stated in an uncharacteristic snarl.

I glared at him. "She was trying to be helpful."

"By hooking you up with a stranger?" Maddox mumbled. "That isn't you, Sandy."

I crossed my arms. "I am not hooking up with anyone. I am not on Tinder or any of those other apps that cater to sex for fun. It's a site that helps mature people find others of similar likes to engage in the pleasure of each other's company. It's my life, my decision. You three need to stay out of it."

They stared at me, and I had to bite back a smile. Given how I found the entire process taxing and couldn't even bother checking my matches, I had no idea why I was defending my choice—except that it was *my* choice.

Bentley appeared at my desk, his hair disheveled as if he had run his hands through it repeatedly. "Sandy." He scowled. "We need to talk about this."

I stood and faced them all. "What needs to happen is the four of you go back to your offices and to the business at hand. What I choose to do or not do in my private life is my concern, not yours."

"Your safety—"

"We're worried—"

"So many nutjobs—"

I held up my hand. "Boys. Enough. If I see someone I would like to meet, I would do so in a public place. I would also make sure someone knew where I would be. I would never give out any personal information until I was certain I trusted the individual." I shook my head. "You know me better than to think I would act foolishly."

Bentley spoke, frustration evident in his tone. "By joining one of these sites, you *are* being foolish."

I was done.

I sat down. "Easy for you to say since you go home every night to your family, Bentley. As do all of you. My world changed when Max died, and I'm trying to find my feet again. Meet some new people and perhaps not be alone so much. I am not entirely comfortable with the whole idea, but at least the girls understood and tried to help, instead of acting dismissive and treating me like an old woman who doesn't know what she's doing."

They all had the grace to look ashamed.

Bentley shook his head. "Sandy, we don't think that. We're just worried."

Aiden looked pained. "We want you to be happy, but this scares me."

Maddox grimaced. "You never said anything."

But it was Reid who deflated my anger and brought tears to my eyes. He leaned forward and gripped my hands.

"Come live with Becca and me, Sandy. We won't let you be lonely anymore."

His words and the utter sincerity with which he said them touched my heart. I smiled at them—the small cluster of men standing in front of me, looking as if they were six years old and in trouble for their antics on the playground instead of the successful, take-charge businessmen they were. Their love and concern shone out in their gazes, and the anger I had been feeling dissipated into the air.

"Thank you, Reid. It's a lovely gesture, but not needed. Boys, I'm not doing anything rashly or without thinking. I promise. If I see a profile I'm interested in, I'll have you check them out. All right, Aiden?"

He nodded, looking resigned.

"And I'll be careful."

"Have your cell phone with you," Maddox insisted.

"Always."

"I want to know your schedule," Bentley stated.

I withheld my laughter. "I think that's my job," I teased.

"Please."

"Fine."

"I'm monitoring that site," Reid muttered.

I rolled my eyes.

Aiden bent close. "I'm following you when you go. I'll sit in the background, so I'm not noticed, but I'll be close in case there's trouble."

My lips twitched. *Not noticed.* At 6'7", with muscles everywhere, a vivid tattoo on his arm, and his good looks, Aiden never blended.

"We can all go," Maddox offered.

I burst into laughter, envisioning the look on some poor man's face when I sat across from him to have a coffee and the boys sat at the table behind me, glaring in his direction, Aiden cracking his knuckles, Reid somehow hacking in to his phone and digging into his background, while Maddox demanded financial reports, and Bentley stared him down.

How fun.

As I laughed, I met the gaze of Van Morrison, who had come in with Bentley but stayed back from my desk. He listened to the conversation, a smile playing on his lips. As he met my gaze, he gave me a thumbs-up and mouthed the words, "You go, Sandy," before disappearing down the hall.

At least he didn't give me a hassle, and I appreciated his silent support.

I brought my attention back to my gang of protectors.

"Good ideas. I'll let you know. Now, back to work, boys."

Grumbling, they disappeared into Bentley's office, shutting the door behind them. I knew I hadn't heard the last of this, but I wasn't surprised by their reaction.

I looked down at my phone, weary of the constant beeps. I scanned through the profiles, knowing deep in my heart this wasn't the right step for me.

But I wasn't telling them that.

Not yet.

THREE

JORDAN

I glanced at my desk with a deep exhale. The paperwork was astronomical these days. The busier BAM became, the busier I was. Even though Bentley had hired an extra body to help me, my desk never seemed to clear. I oversaw all paperwork on every project BAM undertook. Every permit, plan, license, contract that was required for a project, I made sure it was in place. It was a never-ending task, given the vast number of endeavors the company had on the go at any one time.

I pulled off my glasses and rubbed my tired eyes. I drained my coffee and sat back for a moment, contemplating the piles on my desk. I had come in on the weekend to catch up, but there was still a large amount of work to get done.

Not that I had anything else to keep me busy. My daughter, Gina, had recently moved, and with the absence of her and my grandkids—and my son, Warren, already on the other side of the country—life was emptier now than ever. For the first time since my wife, Anna, had passed, I was lonely. When she was alive and our kids here, we had been busy with work, each other, plus the grandkids and all their activities. When she died, my kids tried hard to keep me busy. Now that they were gone, I missed them all. My single son's job had ended, and he had to go to where the work was, so he moved to Alberta last year. Three months ago, my daughter's husband, Eric, had been offered a fabulous promotion, but it meant relocation. And although Gina had expressed her fears over leaving me, I had refused to be the reason they didn't take the opportunity. I promised lots of visits, and although I spoke with her or the kids almost daily, it wasn't the same. Life was hollower.

I had lots of free time on my hands, so I spent it in the office. There was usually someone else around, so I didn't feel as lonely as when I was rambling around my house.

On occasion, the extra time in the office meant I got to see more of Sandy Preston as well.

The right-hand to all the partners, Sandy was an amazing woman. Close in age, we had a lot in common. She was intelligent, driven, and kind—easy to like, and I had a deep, abiding respect for her. She had been a good friend to me when Anna had passed, and when Sandy lost Max, I returned the favor—understanding the tremendous pain she felt. We had coffee together, even the occasional lunch, and we could discuss the loss of our partners freely, both of us having experienced the grieving process.

But as time went by, I began to look at her differently. I no longer saw her as the efficient, friendly coworker and/or friend I'd considered her to be all these years. The fellow grief-stricken companion. I found myself no longer wanting to talk only about Anna or to feel sad. I wanted to talk to Sandy about other things. To expand the friendship beyond loss and into *living*.

But I wasn't sure she was ready for that, and if sensing that my feelings were changing, she had quietly stopped our coffee dates without even discussing it. She was still friendly and cordial in the office. Always smiling and happy to chat if I dropped by her desk or she was bringing me more paperwork, but there was a line there. Because of my respect for her, it was a line I didn't cross.

She was too good a friend to lose. I hoped if I was patient enough, one day she would be ready to move on. And when she was, I would be ready.

Yet, seeing her everyday caused an odd ache in my chest that never fully went away.

I shook my head at my strange thoughts and pushed my glasses back up on my face. I picked up my pen, ready to attack the next set of paperwork when Van Morrison, our resident genius of the hammer, strolled in. He unloaded a huge pile of tools in the corner, then made me frown as he shut the door to the hall and sat at his desk.

Van never shut the door unless there was a problem.

"What's up?" I asked.

He scrubbed his face and regarded me seriously. "I know we don't get overly personal here, Jordan, but Liv told me something last night, and I've been thinking it over all day."

"Damn it," I cursed. "Is there a problem? Is she thinking of leaving?"

He laughed. "No. She's good. *We're* good," he emphasized.

He and Liv were in a relationship that worked well for them. They were a great couple and were getting married soon. Van adored her daughter, and together, they fit. I relaxed. "Okay. So, what is this news?"

He inhaled. "I need to ask you something, and I need you to be honest."

I frowned. "Always."

"Sandy," he said flatly. "You like her."

"Doesn't everyone?" I asked, unsure where this was leading.

"Yes. But you like her as more than a coworker."

I blew out a long breath. "That obvious, am I?"

He shook his head. "No. But you forget how well I know you." He lifted an eyebrow in a silent question, still waiting for my answer.

"Yes, I like her. Very much so."

"I thought so."

"So your news has to do with Sandy?" A flash of panic hit me. "Oh god. Is she seeing someone?"

Had I waited too long?

"Not yet," he said slowly.

"Not yet? What does that mean?" I asked, confused.

Van leaned forward. "It means, if you truly have feelings for her, now is the time for you to speak up."

Van's words replayed in my head. Over and again.

Sandy had signed up on a dating site.

Sandy.

Dating site.

Somehow the words did not compute.

Sandy was too elegant. Too amazing to put herself out there that way. My son used dating apps a lot. Some of his stories made me shudder. The thought of Sandy being subjected to strange men didn't sit well with me.

The thought of her liking someone else besides me in that fashion didn't sit well either.

I sat at my desk long after Van had left. He didn't have a lot to tell me except the name of the dating site and the amusing reaction the partners had when they discovered that their Sandy was putting herself out there.

"It was as if she was a child." He chuckled. "They surrounded her, lecturing and pointing out every bad thing they could think of when it came to dating sites. All of them—even Bentley—were freaked out."

"I don't imagine that went over well with Sandy."

Van shook his head, his eyes crinkling in laughter. "She told them all off in perfect Sandy fashion. One second they were all talking, the next they were all shuffling their feet and looking embarrassed. She put them in their place fast." He paused. "But you could feel her love for them. She knew they were doing this out of concern. But she pointed out it was her life and she had to choose how to live it. She also reminded them they all had spouses or girlfriends to go home to each night." He fell silent. "Even I heard the pain in her voice then. They backed off but made her promise to be very careful."

I shook my head to clear my thoughts. I could see Sandy, drawing herself up, straightening her shoulders as she faced off with "her boys." She loved them all fiercely, and they returned that love. They were very good to her, and she was much more than an assistant to them. But she never hesitated to call them out when she felt they were wrong, and I knew she wouldn't be happy being told what to do.

But I agreed with them.

I turned to the computer and downloaded the app Van told me she had joined. I checked the rules, figured out how it worked, and created an account. A picture was optional—you could have a description only if you preferred, then choose to share a picture with any matches if you decided you wanted to connect. I chose that option, adding a fast bio and a password.

Then I scanned the pages, looking over the profiles.

I stopped scrolling when I came to Sandy's picture. I glanced at the stats, my eyebrows shooting up in shock when I saw how many stars she had beside her profile. There was a tremendous amount of interest in her.

Not that I could blame them. The picture of her was taken at a BAM function. Her hair was down, the bright white gleaming under the lights. Her lovely hazel eyes twinkled in the photo, her full mouth smiling as she looked toward something past the lens that had caught her attention. She was a striking woman. Her confidence and friendly disposition only added to her attractiveness. She had a lot to offer the right man—but the simple fact was, the right man wasn't on this site.

Even though there were a lot of men wanting to get to know her better, I smiled in grim satisfaction that Sandy had yet to return any interest stars.

I sat in front of my laptop, thinking. I had two choices. Reach out via this dating app and see what happened, or simply present myself to her exactly the way her profile requested—as a fellow human feeling lonely and wanting some companionship. Maybe if she spent some time with me, things could develop between us. We were already friends with a lot in common—surely the next step wouldn't be that difficult to work toward?

If she was ready. I had the feeling that would be the largest hurdle to overcome. I had reached a point in my life where I felt I would like to share my time with someone again. The question was—had Sandy?

I shut down the laptop, not bothering with anything else to do with the app.

I knew what I had to do.

SANDY

A couple of days later, I gathered some files and headed upstairs to meet with Bentley. I straightened my tie, brushed the sleeves of my suit jacket, and checked the mirror to make sure my hair was in place.

Van chuckled from his desk, not even looking up. "You look great. Go get her, tiger."

I didn't bother denying my task. "I'm asking her to lunch after my meeting."

"Good."

"I'm hoping she'll say yes."

"I imagine you are."

"It's just lunch. We've had lunch together many times."

"Yes, you have."

"It's not a big deal."

Van's amusement was obvious. "If you're trying to convince me, I'm good. I think it's Sandy you need to save the arguments for."

I sighed. "I'm so rusty at this."

He sat back, looking at me. "Be her friend, Jordan. You two have so much in common, and you've always gotten on well. Just be Jordan and see what happens. I think you'll be surprised."

"Okay."

"She told Liv she planned on deleting the app. She said it wasn't for her. So, this is a good time."

The news buoyed my spirit. "Good. Thanks."

I tucked the files under my arm and headed upstairs.

Sandy was at her desk, busy with one of the many tasks she took care of. But she looked up as I stepped off the elevator, her smile warm. I noticed she looked a little tired, although she was still lovely. Her hair was swept up in its usual chignon, and her outfit was impeccable, the deep blue of the suit setting off her white hair and coloring to perfection. She looked younger than her fifty-seven years, her face unlined, and her figure tight and pleasing to my eyes. She was young at heart, her smiles easy and her attitude positive. She was also incredibly organized and ran the office brilliantly. The boys would be lost without her. I enjoyed watching her run circles around them.

I grinned as I stopped in front of her desk.

"Morning, Sandy."

"Jordan," she replied with a brief nod. "Bentley's still tied up on a call. He'll be free in a few moments."

"Great. I'll grab a coffee."

She stood. "I was getting myself one."

"Then we can get them together." I set down my files and followed her to the small kitchen. I admired the way her hips swayed as she walked in front of me, her scent drifting on the air as she moved. It was citrusy and light. Feminine. I liked it.

She poured two cups of coffee, handing me mine. I sipped the hot liquid with appreciation.

"You make a great cup of coffee, Sandy."

She added some cream to her cup, stirring it. "Thanks."

I leaned my hip on the counter, trying to appear casual. "How's it going? We haven't caught up in a while."

She mimicked my stance, blowing on the hot brew before taking a sip. I tried not to notice how full her lips looked as she puckered them, but I failed. I wondered, not for the first time, how her mouth would feel underneath mine. How she would feel in my arms.

I startled when I realized she had replied, and I had missed it.

"Sorry," I muttered. "I just thought of something I needed to remember to ask Bentley."

"No problem. I said I was fine, and yes, it's been a while."

I said the words before I could chicken out. "How about we rectify that?"

"Sorry?"

"Lunch. I forgot to bring my lunch today, so I was going to get something and sit in the park since it's such a nice day. Join me, and we can catch up over a sandwich."

She hesitated and I smiled.

"I know you're busy—we both are. But it's a lovely day outside, and we can take a break and share a sandwich. Catch up. I miss our coffee breaks." I went in for the kill, remembering her words on her profile.

Seeking companionship—a friend to enjoy life's moments with.

"We need to grab nice days like today and spend time with good friends."

Her brow furrowed then cleared. "I'd like that."

Internally, I high-fived myself. Outwardly, I smiled and nodded. "Great. I'll meet you downstairs about twelve?"

"Yes."

I turned and headed back to her desk, not wanting her to see the large grin I was sporting. I was looking forward to lunch—and whatever came after it.

FOUR

JORDAN

Bentley finished signing the stack of forms I had given him. "You've been busy, Jordan."

I chuckled. "Not as if I had much choice. You're acquiring projects faster than I can keep up."

He closed the file, handing it back to me. "Is Alan not helping you enough?"

"No, he's great. He keeps up with the filing, copying, all the small things I don't have to worry about so I can concentrate on getting all the paperwork in place and assigning crews. Still—" I grinned "— you're a busy man, which makes my job busy. And secure."

Bentley relaxed back in his chair, regarding me seriously. "You never have to worry about your job, Jordan. Or your retirement."

The partners had given me an unexpected gift on my fifty-fifth birthday. A generous retirement package I could start drawing on at sixty years of age. I hadn't reached that milestone yet and had no interest in retiring in the near future, and the partners were quite vocal in their desire for me to stay as long as I wanted with the firm. It was typical of BAM and the men who ran the company. They looked after their own. I had never known a company as well run and generous as BAM. Bentley, Aiden, and Maddox were, in my opinion, the model all companies should strive to be. Turnover here was rare, given how well they treated their staff—right down to the IT department and the people doing the manual labor for them. No one was too small to be taken care of. I was proud to be associated with them, and as I worked with many outside companies, I knew how highly regarded they were within the business industry.

"I know and appreciate it, Bentley. You seem to be on a bit of a streak at the moment."

He laughed, the amusement softening the sternness of his features. Known as serious and businesslike, Bentley only showed his softer side to those who knew him best—and none knew him more than his wife, Emmy, who brought out a side of Bentley I never knew existed. When his daughter was born, another side emerged—the protective, loving father. It also seemed to amplify his professional zeal, and he was constantly buying up properties and land for development. Our construction crews had grown, new foremen and workers hired on. Van and his crew had just completed the renos on a new building that would house the ever-growing group of men that now worked for BAM. Van was going to be moving to the new building, and I was going to miss him as an office mate, although I would be spending a lot of time there as well. Luckily, it was only down the block from the main building so it was a short walk and I would see him often. I was sure he'd still be here a fair deal, but the space was needed.

"I'll try to rein myself in," he joked. "Not sure if that will happen or not. I found another piece of property in the Niagara region. It's not protected this time, and it would make an awesome condo project. The views will command a steep price. I have an architect working on the concept."

There was a soft knock, then Sandy stuck her head in the door. "Bentley, your one o'clock canceled. Did you want me to get you lunch?"

He glanced at his calendar. "Please. Can you reschedule my three o'clock in earlier? Maybe I could get home and surprise Emmy. We could take Addi to the park."

"Already done."

He beamed at her. "Thanks, Sandy."

"Turkey on rye?"

"Yes."

"Jordan, I'll get our lunch at the same time. Corned beef, hot mustard, with extra pickles on the side, right?"

"Perfect."

"I'll get us sodas and a cookie as a treat."

The door shut, and I turned back to Bentley, who was watching me, his eyes narrowed in curiosity.

"Having lunch with Sandy?" he asked, trying to act casual and failing. Miserably.

I nodded, gathering up my files. "Yes. It's a lovely day. I thought we'd have a sandwich in the park. Get out of the office for a bit and clear our heads."

"Good idea."

"I thought so."

"So, it's just...*lunch?*"

"It's two friends having lunch, yes."

He drummed his fingers on the desk, then cleared his throat and tugged on his shirt sleeves. All three were tells for Bentley when he was thinking or worried.

"It's lunch, Bentley," I said quietly. "And anything else is private."

"*Is* there something else?"

I met his gaze directly, my voice firm. "That is up to Sandy, and not something I will discuss."

His eyebrows shot up, and then he smiled.

"I understand."

"Good."

I respected Bentley—all the partners—but this was private. And right now, it was nothing but lunch. The last thing either Sandy or I needed was a lecture. That would end anything before it began—that much I knew. Sandy was private and would hate it, so it wasn't up for discussion.

"I'm very fond of Sandy," he murmured. "We all are."

"I'm aware."

"She's been having a hard time lately."

I nodded.

"I think lunch with a friend is a great idea."

I said nothing.

He smiled, his voice quiet when he spoke. "I think with the right person, *something else*—which of course would remain private—would

32

be a wonderful thing. Between two people who care about each other, it's always a wonderful thing."

I wanted to laugh at his unsubtle but well-meaning speech. Instead, I remained impassive.

I stood. "Anything else, Bentley?"

He shook his head, still smiling. "No."

I headed to the door.

"Jordan."

I turned, my hand on the knob. "Yes?"

"Have a good lunch. Take a little extra time. As you said, it's a lovely day. Enjoy it."

I couldn't help my grin. "Thanks, Bentley. We'll do that."

Sandy and I walked to the park behind the BAM building. I carried the bag containing our lunch, and we chatted about the office as we walked. I indicated an empty picnic bench, and we headed toward it.

I handed Sandy the bag and used my handkerchief to wipe the dust from her seat and the top of the table, then laid it on the bench before she sat down.

"What a gentleman," she murmured.

"I would hate to see that pretty suit get dirty. It's one of my favorites."

She lifted her eyebrows. "*One* of your favorites?"

I unpacked the bag, setting out the food. "Yes. Only one of many."

Sandy studied me. "Which are your others?"

I took a bite of my sandwich, chewing and swallowing, then sipping the cold soda to chase away the hot mustard.

"All the blue ones, the green, and that lovely rust-colored dress you wear. I like you in bold colors. They suit you."

She blinked. Took a bite of her roast beef sandwich and chewed. Frowned and took another bite, then replied.

"I have no idea what to say to that, Jordan. I didn't realize you noticed what I wore. Certainly not enough to have favorites."

I opened the container of carrot and celery sticks she had ordered and chomped on one before replying.

"I do notice, Sandy. It's hard not to. You are a beautiful woman. I enjoy looking at you."

She stared at me, wordless.

I shrugged. "I'm simply stating a fact."

"I see."

I decided to go for broke. I wanted to lay my cards on the table and see how she reacted. I had played it safe before, and it went nowhere.

"With your beautiful hair and captivating eyes, it gives me a lot of pleasure to watch you." Then I winked. "You have great legs. I love it when your skirts are a bit shorter."

This time, she gaped. She set down her sandwich and wiped her fingers. "If I didn't know better, I'd say you were flirting with me, Jordan Hayes."

"I am."

"I thought this was friends having lunch."

"We are friends," I insisted. "We're having lunch." I drew in a long breath. "But who's to say there can't be more?"

"More?" she repeated.

I finished my sandwich and wadded up the wrapper, slipping it back into the bag.

"Please eat, Sandy. You are far too thin these days."

A soft flush of color drifted across her cheeks. It was rare I ever saw her blush, but the color complemented and highlighted her delicate beauty. But she picked up her sandwich and ate.

"I was honest when I told you I missed our coffee breaks together, Sandy. You ended them, and I always wondered why."

"I thought it was time to move on from our sad sessions," she confessed.

"I did as well. Why didn't you say so?"

She shrugged. "I wasn't sure how to. I thought...I thought you would think I was being disrespectful to our spouses. To their memories. We were getting closer and it felt—wrong somehow."

"Why? Because you were ready to look forward and not behind you anymore? Did you think I would be upset by that?"

She sighed. "It's complicated, Jordan."

"Life is complicated. All of it. But it's meant to be lived." I rested my elbows on the table, clasping my hands together loosely. "I think both Anna and Max would want us to move forward. It's been a long time for both of us, Sandy." I paused. "Isn't that what you were trying to do with Mature Matchups?"

Her eyes widened. "You know about that?"

"Van told me."

"Why would he do that?"

I met her gaze. "Because he knew I wanted to ask you out. Not as a friend having a sandwich in the park, but a proper date. I held back because I wasn't sure you were ready, but when he told me, I knew I had to step forward before I lost you to some jerk-off on a dating app who doesn't deserve you."

A smile tugged on her lips. "I'm sure they're not all jerk-offs."

"Have you seen the profiles? Jesus, Sandy, even at our age, they all want one thing—and it's not companionship. I'm pretty sure the Viagra manufacturers sponsor those sites."

"Well then, at our age, as you so delightfully put it, there would be a lot of short relationships. Or a huge surge in the Viagra market—which apparently would lead to a different kind of surge—at least temporarily so."

Then she laughed, trying to cover it up with her hand. I started to laugh with her, relieved at her teasing.

I risked it and reached for her hand. She let me wrap mine around hers, the softness of her skin warm under my touch. "Don't go on a date with anyone on that site, Sandy. Let me take you out."

"On a date?"

I laughed. "If that sounds too scary, then let's just go to dinner and a movie. Or dinner and a show. A walk. Whatever you want."

"It sounds as if dinner is nonnegotiable."

"It is."

"We work together."

"And BAM has no policies against interoffice relationships. Hell, half the office is dating or married to each other, it seems."

She laid her free hand on top of our joined fingers. "I don't want to lose our friendship."

"I don't think we'll lose anything, Sandy. All I'm asking is for us to have a meal together. Spend some time together outside the office. I think we're both lonely." I sighed. "I haven't been out with anyone since Anna passed. I don't even know if I'm ready. But I do know this, if there is anyone I would like to try with, it's you."

"Why?" she asked quietly.

"Because you're beautiful. I'm not talking only your outside beauty. I'm talking about the person you are. Kind, smart, funny. You're warm and loving. Sweet. And as alone as I am." I squeezed her hand. "We're both too young to be alone. I think we have a lot to offer the other person. And if we decide it's only as friends, then so be it. But I want to explore it. Try it. With you. If you're willing."

She looked over my shoulder, thinking. I let her process my words. I hadn't planned on jumping in so quickly, but it had happened naturally, and I wasn't upset by my words.

As long as she didn't turn me down.

Her eyes met mine, and something inside me settled. Her gaze was warm and open and when she replied, my heart soared.

"I would love to go on a date with you, Jordan."

I lifted her hand to my mouth and kissed her knuckles.

"Thank you."

SANDY

I threw yet another dress on the bed and huffed out an exasperated sigh. Nothing I tried on felt right. I looked at the pile on the mattress and wondered if perhaps the reason for that was because each dress I tried had somehow had a memory linked to Max. A dinner we went out to. The night he took me dancing as a surprise before the disease put him in that damn wheelchair. The nights I would dress up and we would share an evening together at home on a "date."

I sat down, shaking my head. I couldn't do this. I wasn't ready to date another man. Even though Jordan told me to think of it as two friends sharing a meal, I knew what it actually was.

I saw the interest in his eyes when we talked yesterday. The pitch of his voice, the way he held my hand, his frank words—none of that said *friend*.

I reached for my phone to call and cancel, then stopped as his words to me yesterday came back.

"By the way, Sandy, I won't be taking any calls or messages from you tomorrow. I know you'll have second thoughts, and you'll try to cancel. Not happening. We're going out for dinner. Accept it and maybe, just maybe, you'll enjoy it." Then he winked and left the office.

I knew Jordan and his gentle ways. If I called, he would answer, and he would take my decision because that was how he worked. He would be disappointed, but he would accept it, and the next time I saw him at work, treat me no differently from any other day.

I dropped my phone back on the bed. I wasn't sure I was ready, but I wasn't sure I wasn't ready.

I laughed out loud at my thoughts. Even they were confused.

Jordan Hayes was a wonderful man. We had been friends since he started at BAM. He lost his wife, Anna, over four years ago, and for a while, lost himself as well. It took him a long time to recover from his grief, and when Max died, our common bond of losing a spouse brought us closer. He was easy to talk to and understood my grief. We shared many stories, laughter, and tears, and his friendship brought me great comfort.

He was right—I did end our biweekly coffee breaks because I thought we were getting too close. Too familiar. I started to depend on those outings and seeing him, and I felt guilty. Disloyal to Max that I could already need another man's presence in my life. So I simply stopped the outings. I remained friendly and cordial, but after inventing reasons not to go out for coffee, Jordan got the message and backed off.

Until this past week.

I stood and rehung the dresses I had been trying on back in the closet. I always did my best thinking while my hands were busy.

Jordan drifted through my mind. He was a tall man, his shoulders still straight and wide. His hair was gray, but thick and wavy. He kept it neat and brushed back from his face, and he was usually clean-shaven, although he sported neatly trimmed scruff at times which suited his strong jawline. He wore glasses for reading, his frames setting off his intense green eyes. He preferred dress pants and button-down shirts, the sleeves often rolled up, showing off his fore-arms. It was rare he wore a suit, but when he did, he wore it well. He was quiet and unflappable, meticulous in his work habits, and well respected in the office. He was always willing to lend a hand, work extra, or pitch in on whatever needed doing. He was well thought of by the partners, and the feelings went both ways—he thought highly of all of them. They called him the *King of Paperwork* and relied on him for his unfailing dedication.

He was a great man. Thoughtful, kind, and sweet. He always remembered birthdays, had a kind word to say to people, and encour-aged those around him.

And I had liked the way his hand felt wrapped around mine the other day.

I hung the last dress and made a decision. I was going on this non-date date, and I needed a new dress to do so.

I picked up my purse and glanced at my watch. It was only two, and Jordan wasn't picking me up until seven.

I could do this.

FIVE

SANDY

I opened the door promptly at seven and met Jordan's warm gaze. My constant plaguing doubts faded away as he regarded me. With a smile, he held out a bunch of irises. He leaned forward and brushed my cheek with his lips.

"You take my breath away, Sandy."

I accepted the flowers, touched he remembered irises were my favorites, and stepped back. "Come in while I put these in water." I walked toward the kitchen, calling over my shoulder. "Would you like a drink?"

He followed me, stopping in the doorway as I filled a vase and arranged the flowers. "No thanks, I'm good. I'll have some wine with dinner."

"All right."

"New dress?"

I felt myself blush. "Yes, it is."

He stepped closer—close enough, I felt the heat of him at my back. "For me?" he asked quietly.

My heart rate picked up, and all I could do was nod. As soon as I saw the simple, deep-blue dress, I knew it was perfect. It skimmed my breasts, fluttered around my knees, and the scooped neck was elegant yet sexy. It felt like me, and the color, Jordan had admitted the other day, one of his favorites.

He settled his hands on my shoulders and turned me around. Our eyes met, gentle green holding my nervous hazel, and he smiled. "Thank you."

"You're welcome."

"Ready to go to dinner?"

I drew in some much-needed oxygen. My stomach fluttered, and my breathing had picked up at his closeness. It felt odd...yet right. "Yes."

He crooked his arm. "Then let's go."

I set down my wine, laughing. "I wish I had seen that."

Jordan chuckled, wiping his eyes. "It was amusing. Van always makes me laugh. But watching him carry Liv out over one shoulder and Sammy over the other—all while Liv was giving him shit about something and Sammy was pretending to be queen of the castle and calling him Prince Van? It was priceless." He shook his head. "I'm going to miss having him around every day."

"He'll be in and out, I'm sure. Bentley is constantly needing him for something."

"Thank goodness for that."

The waiter appeared, removing our plates. Dinner had been...fun. More fun than I could recall having in a very long time. The food was excellent, the wine superb, and the company perfect. Jordan was charming, funny, courteous, and the most gracious of dinner companions. We'd shared an appetizer, tasted each other's meals, and talked the entire time. There was no awkwardness or stilted moments. The evening simply flowed.

I perused the dessert menu with a sigh. "I think I'm too full."

"Nonsense," Jordan exclaimed. "There is always room for dessert."

"Says the man with the sweet tooth."

He grinned. "I do have that. Anna used to keep baked goods on hand for me all the time. I constantly raided the cookie jar."

I chuckled. "Max was the same. He never met a dessert he didn't like."

"Smart guy. Now, what looks good?"

I smiled as I went back to looking at the menu. There was nothing strange about talking about our spouses with each other. Other people tended to shy away from even mentioning Max's name, yet Jordan had no issues at all. It didn't bother me to hear him speak of Anna either. They were huge parts of our past lives, and it seemed almost natural to bring them into the conversation at times.

"The crème brûlée looks good," I mused.

He closed his menu. "So does the chocolate mousse. Share?"

"Lovely."

"Then we can take a stroll and walk off some of these calories. All right?"

"Yes."

A gentle breeze blew across my face as we walked along the docks at the marina. Boats bobbed in the water, the hulls bumping against the wood. We stood and admired a few boats on the harbor, the lights on their masts glimmering in the water. Jordan had offered me his hand when he helped me out of the car, and it had remained wrapped around mine as we strolled along the docks.

"Do you like boats, Sandy?"

I furrowed my brow. "I don't dislike them. I haven't been on one very often, to be honest. Max and I went on a cruise once. I liked it, but he wasn't a fan. Other than that, we did a tour of the harbor one time, and I think we went on a friend's boat once."

"Not a water lover, I guess?"

I chuckled. "You could say that. I can't even begin to describe the shades of green he turned. Even with medication."

Jordan laughed. "Poor Max."

"He tried. But it was never something we could do together, and it wasn't any fun doing it on my own."

"Hmph. I'll have to change that for you."

"Oh? You like boats?"

He stopped in front of a small, neat sailboat. It gleamed white under the lights, the deck a dark contrast to the color of the boat. "I do. This one is mine. I take her out whenever I can."

"I didn't know that about you."

He turned to me with a smile. "That's the point of dating someone, Sandy. You get to know all about them." He winked. "Try before you buy sort of thing."

I laughed. "I'm a little out of practice."

"So am I. But I think we're doing pretty damn well so far, don't you?"

I had to agree. Once I had set aside my nerves, the evening had gone well. Better than well. I had thoroughly enjoyed myself.

He stepped onto the deck, holding out his hand. "Come aboard."

I stumbled getting into the boat, and Jordan's arms shot out to steady me. He pulled me tight to his chest, and for a minute I felt him. Solid, warm, safe.

Then he stepped back. "Okay now?"

I brushed back my hair self-consciously. "Sorry—not a very graceful move on my part."

He reached over and tucked a stray strand behind my ear. His fingers seemed to linger, then he lowered his arm. "I love it when you wear your hair down," he murmured. "It's beautiful."

"Thank you," I breathed out.

For a moment, we stared at each other, a warmth pulsating in the air around us. Then he smiled and stepped back.

"We'll get your sea legs under you soon enough. Now come see my little boat."

I didn't know a lot about boats, but Jordan's was very pretty. Lots of wood and bright plaid in the small cabin made it feel warm and cozy. He showed me the tiny galley, the compact bathroom, and the bed hidden behind a long curtain that doubled as a seating area. It was all neat, tidy, and comfortable looking, albeit tiny.

I was surprised to find out the boat wasn't named after his wife. He shook his head when I asked. "Anna hated the water. She didn't get ill like Max, she just hated it. She didn't swim or like to go to the beach, and she never once came on the boat. So, I named it after my favorite kind of day to have on it. *Open Waters.*"

"Oh."

"A good friend of Anna's drowned when they were younger—she witnessed it happen. She never got over it."

"How terrible."

"It was for her—she was never able to move past it. So, I had the boat, and she had her quilting and sewing. I didn't understand that and she didn't like this, but it was fine. We both had something we loved." He smiled. "As I discovered, it's okay to have different interests, even when you're married. We were never one of those couples who had to do everything together."

I nodded in understanding. "As we got older, Max and I were the same. He worked so much he hated to leave the house when he had time off. He liked to hang around the house, take some time to write one of his books or a paper. I loved to travel, so we came up with a compromise. We'd stagger our vacations, and I would hang with him at the house for a week, then take a short trip with one of the grandkids or a friend. When he was working, I stayed busy with book clubs and different activities. We went on the occasional trip, but he loved resorts and I loved to explore. We took turns."

"We both had great spouses."

I smiled warmly at him. "We did."

He cocked his head, studying me. "I think they'd be okay with us, out together tonight."

I thought of Max. All the conversations we'd had over the course of his illness. He'd met Jordan a few times and always thought he was a nice man.

"*Classy,*" he said one day. "*That man has class.*"

My voice was low when I responded. "I think you're right."

I was quiet on the drive home. Jordan seemed lost in thought as well but was still solicitous, opening my door, helping me into the passenger seat, making sure I was warm enough. The silence wasn't uncomfortable, but contemplative.

When we arrived at the house, Jordan walked me to the door, waiting until I unlocked it. I suddenly felt nervous. Tense.

Jordan met my eyes, a look of understanding on his face. "I had a lovely evening, Sandy." He gazed at me. "I would like to repeat it."

"Another date?"

"Yes."

"I'd like that."

His eyes lit up. "Great."

He leaned forward and my heartbeat skyrocketed. My shoulders stiffened, and I drew in a sharp breath. He turned his head and his warm lips brushed against my cheek, then he stepped back, his face inscrutable. "Sleep well, Sandy. I'll see you at the office on Monday. But if it's okay, maybe I'll call tomorrow?"

I nodded, mumbling an agreement. His smile was gentle, and he stroked down my cheek with the backs of his knuckles.

"Good night."

I stumbled inside, shutting the door and leaning against it, shocked at the disappointment that flooded my body. My reaction to his closeness wasn't one of rejection, but one of anticipation.

I had *wanted* him to kiss me.

He thought I was saying no. And Jordan, being Jordan, accepted it with understanding and grace.

I spun around and flung open the door, prepared to hurry down the steps before he drove off.

Except he was standing where I left him. Waiting outside my door as if he couldn't bear to leave. Our gazes locked and held.

"I wanted to kiss you," he said. "But you didn't want that. Did I ruin the evening with the comment about Anna and Max?"

"No. I love that we can talk about them."

"But you didn't want me to kiss you." It was a statement this time, not a question.

"I did," I replied. "I was just nervous and worried and—"

He didn't let me finish. In one step, he was in front of me, his hands cupping my face, his fingers tender and warm against my skin. He kissed my forehead, my cheeks, across the bridge of my nose, nudging at it with his own as he discovered me with his lips. Then sweetly, gently, his mouth settled on mine, and he kissed me.

He slipped his hands down my arms, winding his arms around my waist as he pulled me close. I wrapped mine around his neck, holding tight. He was patient, kissing me through my tremors, waiting until I relaxed. Then his kiss deepened, his tongue sliding along my bottom lip, asking for entrance. He tasted like chocolate and cinnamon. His lips were soft, his tongue like velvet on mine. His arms became a warm sanctuary, his mouth worshiping mine with the most tender of possession. I felt his adoration in his kiss. The thrill of *him* raced through my body, sending shivers of pleasure over me, right down to my toes curling in delight and my fingers gripping his thick hair.

When he eased back, he dropped two light kisses to my mouth, then simply held me. I felt his rapid heartbeat, and I knew he could feel mine. Finally, he kissed my forehead and stepped away. I immediately missed his warmth. He smiled and drew a finger down my cheek.

"Thank you for a perfect evening, Sandy." He lifted my hand and kissed it. "I look forward to many more."

I blinked, unable to form words.

"I'll wait until I hear the door lock behind me."

I stepped backward, our gaze never wavering as I shut the door, turning the lock.

His footsteps faded as he went down the stairs, and I flung open the door again. He turned to look over his shoulder.

"Text me when you get home."

His smile lit the night. "I will. Now, back inside."

I shut the door, smiling when I realized he hadn't moved yet. I snapped the lock, then watched out the window as he left and drove away.

I was still smiling when his text came through.

I am home and already missing you. Thank you for a wonderful night. Sleep well.

Monday suddenly felt very far away.

SIX

JORDAN

I woke on Sunday, my first thought that of Sandy. I stared out the window at the rising sun, remembering the evening, the laughter and teasing. The excitement in her eyes when she was on my boat. I was already planning on taking her out for the day. It was the perfect place to spend time with her. Something I loved, that wasn't as connected to my past. Anna had never even stepped foot on the deck, she was so terrified of water. She had seen a picture and that was all. The boat, my *Open Waters*, would be a great place for me to spend time with Sandy, creating our own memories.

I also thought about our kiss. I thought I'd ruined the evening, and her reaction as I moved in closer seemed negative, so I had backed off. When she'd opened the door, I saw the same desire in her eyes as I was feeling, and I took full advantage of the moment.

I closed my eyes, thinking how Sandy had felt in my arms. It had been so long since I'd held a woman in my embrace that way. She was soft and yielding. Warm. She smelled like citrus and flowers—a delicate fragrance that was enticing and light. And when our mouths had met, the passion that coursed through my body was hot and bright. It still lingered, and my cock, which had been dormant for years, lay hot and heavy against my stomach, growing harder the more I thought of Sandy. It had taken everything I had not to deepen the kiss last night, shut the door behind me and stay with her. Kiss her until she begged for more and then make love to her.

But that was too fast, and I knew we would both regret it. Sandy wasn't a fast flash for me. I already felt something for her—the feelings had been there longer than I was ready to admit to myself, but they were there. Last night had been the first time in years I hadn't felt alone. The first time in many years I felt something other than sadness with only memories to smile about. It was as if I were waking up after a dormant period, my senses coming back to life, yearning to live again.

I slid my hand down my torso, wrapping it around my hard shaft, a low groan escaping as I stroked myself. It had been a long time for me.

It appeared that more than just my senses were waking up.

I threw back the covers and made my way to the shower.

It was time to see just how awake I was.

I sipped my coffee, staring out into the backyard. I sighed, thinking about opening the pool, wondering if I would even bother this year. With Gina and the kids gone, last year, the pool sat mostly unused except for the few times I went in on a particularly hot day. I turned and looked around the house, recalling the conversation I'd had with Gina when they visited at Christmas.

"Have you thought about moving, Dad?" she asked as we went through a box of her mother's belongings that I had put aside for her.

I glanced around the spare room. "At times," I admitted. "How would you feel about that?"

She wrapped up a piece of crystal, sliding it into the box. "It's a house, Dad. I would rather see you happy." She sat down on the bed and took my hand. "You've mentioned rambling around in this place several times. I wondered if maybe it was time to move on."

"Lots of memories here."

She nodded. "The memories, you take with you. Maybe the sad reminders can stay behind."

I had thought a lot about the conversation since then. She was right. I didn't need a house with four bedrooms and twenty-five-hundred square feet to wander around in. I had a service that came in and cleaned the house, but the truth was, eighty percent of it was unused. I had another company come in and do the outside maintenance, but the gardens remained empty aside from the few perennials. Anna had loved gardening, but I was never big on it so had no interest in all the flowers and plants she would add every year, except to admire her handiwork. I had no desire to try to plant anything myself. The thought of another summer of trying to manage it all suddenly seemed a little overwhelming.

The phone rang, and with a smile, I answered. "Hello, Gina. How's my daughter?"

"Good, Dad. How are you?"

"I'm fine. How are Tina and Leo?"

Gina laughed. "Busy. Eric took Leo to soccer this morning, and I'm sitting in the stands while Tina swims."

"I miss them."

"You need to come for another visit."

"I will."

"You sound down, Dad. Are you sure you're okay?"

"Yes. I was thinking about something just before you called."

"What?"

"The conversation we had at Christmas about selling the house."

There was silence, then she spoke. "Are you ready for that?"

"I think I am. It's too big for just me. I don't use the pool anymore, and frankly, I think the house needs a family in it." I rubbed a hand over my eyes. "I think maybe you're right—it's time to move on. You could come and take anything you want—I can ship it out to you. Maybe the dining room set? I know you always loved it. And your mother's china."

"I would love that." She paused. "Has something happened, Dad? Something that made you decide?"

I sat down, unsure what to say. I had always been honest with my kids. "I had a date last night. I think it made me realize it was time to make some changes."

"It must have been some date."

I chuckled. "I've been thinking about moving for a while. I think I realized last night, if I'm ready to move forward in my life, maybe I need a fresh start in other places as well. And to be honest, I'm getting tired of rambling around in this place."

"Too many memories?" she guessed.

I thought about bringing Sandy here. How I would feel being in the house she shared with Max. They would always be in the background. Our past lives. Past loves.

"Good memories, but yes."

"Whatever you think is best, Dad. You know I support you." Then her voice became teasing. "So, this date... You're not suddenly going to spring some young woman on me as an evil stepmom, are you?"

I laughed at her words. "No. The lady I took to dinner was my age. Quite respectable."

"Okay then."

"I'm not looking to replace your mother, sweetheart. I'm just..." I trailed off, unsure what to say.

"I know, Dad. Mom would be happy you are trying. So am I. Warren will be fine with it. You're too young to stay alone for the rest of your life. Just don't rush into anything, okay?"

"I won't. I've known this lady for a long time. We're friends and we went to dinner."

There was another pause. "Was it Sandy?"

I was surprised by her question. "Yes, it was. How did you know?"

"You always talk about her. I sometimes wondered why you didn't ask her out sooner. I figured when you were ready, you would."

"I was waiting for her to be ready."

"Ah, Dad, you're such a gentleman. I love you."

I chuckled. "I love you too."

"I'll have to call you later, and you can tell me all about the date. Tina's lesson is done, and she'll be here in a minute."

"All right, sweetheart. Thanks for calling."

"Okay. Oh, and, Dad..."

"Yes?"

"Thanks for telling me. Remember to practice safe sex. Even at your age!"

Then, laughing, she hung up.

I set down the phone, grinning. I wasn't surprised at Gina's easy acceptance of the changes in my life. We had always been close, and she fussed a lot over me being alone. She had also suggested I sell the house two years ago, but at the time I wasn't ready. At Christmas, I had wavered but decided against it. As I looked around the room, I decided that, perhaps, now I was ready.

———

I checked in with Sandy midafternoon. She answered the call, her voice a little breathless. It immediately took me back to the way she sounded after I had kissed her.

"Hello, Sandy. Having a good day?"

"A busy one. I decided to clean out some spaces. I've filled two garbage bags. Honestly, I have no idea why I had some of this junk stuffed in drawers."

I chuckled. "I know. Sometimes I can't even recall putting things in places."

We shared some amusing stories, the mirth welcome. Then I cleared my throat.

"Thank you again for last night. It was wonderful."

"It was."

"Especially the end."

Her subdued laughter was music to my ears. "That was unexpected, but yes, highly enjoyable."

"Are you free Tuesday?"

"Yes."

"There's a tasting menu at Wallaby's. Each tasting is paired with the perfect wine. Seven courses. How does that sound?"

"Like I might be drunk?"

I snickered. "We'll take a cab, and I'll make sure you get home safe. Would you do me the honor of coming with me?"

"I would love that."

"Great. And Sandy, Van is getting married in a month. Would you come with me as my plus-one?"

"Oh, ah…"

Her hesitation prompted me to ask. "You would prefer not to let people know we're seeing each other?"

"We've only had one date, Jordan."

"Two, after Tuesday, and in a month, it will be so many, you will have lost count."

"You're very sure of yourself."

I couldn't resist teasing her. "I felt your response to my kiss, Sandy. I have every reason to be sure."

"You're such a *rake*." She teased back. "I thought you were a gentleman."

"I'm both."

"I see."

"So?" I pushed. "Tuesday, about twenty more dates, then the wedding? Yes?"

She sighed. "Yes."

I couldn't help my grin. "Perfect."

SANDY

Monday morning, my stomach fluttered with nerves. As I prepared the boardroom for the usual start-of-the-week meeting, I worried about seeing Jordan.

How would he act? Would people know we'd been out together? I valued my privacy and I was certain he did as well, yet I also felt anxious about my reaction to him.

He'd been on my mind all day yesterday. Snippets of our evening came back to me, making me smile as I sorted drawers and tidied the house. The way I felt in his embrace—safe and secure. Surrounded by his scent. Max never wore cologne since many of the hospitals had a fragrance-free policy, so I wasn't used to it, but Jordan smelled like fresh air in the fall—woodsy and warm. I liked it.

And his kiss.

It awakened in me something long dormant. With the age difference between Max and me, our sex life had shifted greatly as Max grew older. The last few years of Max's life, his body had suffered terribly with his MS. He fought it valiantly, but the passion we had shared so strongly throughout our earlier marriage was missing. We snuggled, exchanged whispered words of love, gentle kisses, but that was all. As hard as we tried to prevent it, I became more of a caregiver than his wife, and although I wouldn't have done it any other way, that side of our life was gone.

I touched my mouth, still feeling the pressure of Jordan's lips on mine. The tender possession that had deepened and blossomed into something more. It left me wanting.

And in many ways, it scared me.

Reid walked into the boardroom, his laptop tucked under his arm, a cup of coffee in his hand. He stopped beside me, dropping a kiss to my cheek.

"Hey, Sandy. How was your weekend?"

I patted his cheek. "Good. Yours?"

"Great. Becca and I went shopping for some furniture." He shook his head. "I've never been able to shop for my own stuff before. There're so many choices and decisions. Good thing I have her."

I smiled. "Yes, it is."

Other staff members filed in, and I took my usual place to the side of Bentley. I opened my pad and got ready, knowing once he strode in, the meeting would start. It was as if everyone waited for him, feeding on his energy and leadership to begin the week.

Aiden and Maddox sat down, both smiling and greeting me. My breath caught as Van walked in, followed by Jordan. I relaxed as they both said hello. Jordan smiled, nodded, and sat in his usual place. There was nothing out of the ordinary with his demeanor, nothing overly familiar, yet I felt his glance from across the table. Saw his smile widen a little as I returned his salutation. I averted my eyes as the feeling I was about to blush rushed over me.

Heaven's sake, I hadn't blushed since I was fifteen. What was this man doing to me?

53

Bentley walked in, set his leather-bound journal on the boardroom table, and clapped his hands.

"Morning everyone. We have a busy week ahead of us, so let's get to it."

I was grateful for his briskness this morning. I needed to occupy my hands—and my mind.

Blushing.

What next?

Swooning?

Heaven forbid.

I stayed in my seat, furiously writing the last few moments of the meeting as people filed out. Bentley had been on fire this morning, discussing new projects, the hiring of additional staff, the transition of some people to the new building, as well as a hundred and one other items on his list.

Busy, indeed.

I jotted down some questions I needed to ask, then snapped shut my notepad.

I glanced up, surprised to see all the boys still in their seats. They were all relaxed, sipping coffee, Aiden eating what I was certain was his fourth Danish of the day. I met their glances, confused.

"Boys—what's up?"

"Just checking in, Sandy," Maddox drawled, a smile on his lips.

"Checking in?"

"You look good today," Bentley stated softly. "Lovely as usual, but better."

"I had a nice weekend."

Aiden lifted one eyebrow. "Oh?"

"Very productive. Cleaned out some drawers, went shopping, that sort of thing."

Reid leaned forward. "Anything particularly interesting filed under 'that sort of thing'?"

I rolled my eyes. They were fishing. They knew I had lunch with Jordan last week, and like curious children, they wanted to know what was going on. I stood, brushing off my skirt.

"I deleted that app, if that is what you're wondering. You can all stop worrying."

"We'll never stop worrying about you, Sandy," Bentley stated. "We love you too much."

His words made me smile.

"I'm fine, boys. Carry on with your life."

"Dee and I were out to dinner on Saturday," Maddox said.

I glanced at him, waiting for him to continue.

"Imagine my surprise"—he smirked—"when I saw you across the restaurant, having dinner. With Jordan."

"Imagine," I replied, trying not to laugh. I was incorrect. They were worse than curious children. Four sets of eyes stared at me, all waiting for me to speak.

"The restaurant was lovely. I hope you enjoyed yourself as much as we did," I responded, keeping my voice neutral.

"You looked quite cozy," Maddox added.

"Tell me, how many phone calls happened between the four of you on Sunday? I'm quite shocked none of you was at my door demanding answers yesterday."

They all spoke up at once.

"Emmy wouldn't let me."

"Cami said to leave you alone."

"Dee refused to let me come say hello on Saturday. She told me to give you some privacy."

"Becca told me to butt out."

I picked up my notepad. "Good thing your partners have some sense. Yes, Jordan and I went out for dinner. We had a nice evening. We spoke yesterday on the phone, and we do plan on seeing each other again. Now, I will try to refrain from dragging him into the supply cupboard and having my wicked way with him, and I promise not to make kissy faces at him during meetings, but heaven only knows. He is rather sexy. Now, I believe we're done here."

I swept out of the boardroom, shutting the door behind me. The silence I left was deafening and the shocked looks on their faces priceless.

But I had a feeling I had made my point. I knew that each of them would approach me today and grovel. I planned on enjoying it. I found it quite funny, if I was being honest.

I wasn't angry or even upset. I knew they were all concerned about me, and I also knew they were idiots a great deal of the time when it came to personal matters. Still, I had to set some boundaries.

Even if I loved them all the more for their behavior.

I approached my desk, all other thoughts disappearing when I saw what waited for me. Sitting beside my keyboard was a small vase containing three perfect irises.

There was no note. No indication of who had left them, but I knew who it was.

Jordan.

It was a lovely little reminder of the weekend.

Of him.

The boardroom door opened, and the partners all filed out, heading directly to their offices. They all looked crestfallen, and I was instantly ashamed of berating them.

"Boys," I called softly.

They all turned, looking at me.

"I love you. Interfering idiots you are, that hasn't changed. I promise if I need you, I will call, okay?"

They all smiled in relief, making me chuckle. They couldn't stand it if they felt I was upset—the hard-hearted, tough businessman image they projected was simply that. An image. Underneath their fancy suits and gruff exteriors, they were all caring, loving men—and fiercely protective.

I was glad to be one of the people they cared so deeply about.

"Now, get back to work," I demanded. "I can't do all this myself, you know."

Reid laughed. "I think you do most of it."

I tilted my chin. "Remember that."

They were all sniggering as they dispersed.

I touched the petals on my irises, smiling. I looked up to see Bentley in his doorway, watching me. I winked at him and he grinned.

"I love seeing you smile like that again."

I arched an eyebrow at him, and he lifted his hands in supplication, then disappeared into his office.

I opened my laptop and got to work.

SEVEN

SANDY

Jordan's eyes widened in shock. "Maddox was there? I never noticed him."

I nodded with a grin. "Neither of us did. Apparently, Dee dragged him out of the restaurant and refused to let him interrupt us."

He lifted his wine. "What are the odds?"

"I know."

"Does it bother you? Their interference? Or should I say, attempted interference?" Jordan asked with a smirk. "I love how you shut them down."

I felt the need to defend them. "No, I know how worried they have been. They're just trying to watch out for me."

He leaned across the table, his voice low. "If you still have to prove a point, I'm okay with you dragging me into the storage cupboard." He sat back with a wink. "I'll take one for the team."

I laughed at his humor. "I'll keep that in mind."

"You do that."

The waiter slid a plate in front of us. "Elk ravioli with a blue cheese and thyme cream sauce," he announced, then poured us the next wine pairing. "A rich Syrah with essence of black plum, pepper, and blackberry."

I eyed my plate with anticipation. Everything had been delicious so far. I cut into the pasta and tasted the offering. The richness of the cheese and the dense filling was heaven.

Jordan groaned around his mouthful. "This is amazing."

I sipped the pungent, dry wine with appreciation. It was the perfect accompaniment to the decadent pasta.

"This just gets better and better," I agreed.

We had left the office together, heading straight for the restaurant in a car service Jordan ordered for the night. He planned on taking me home, then having the car drop him off at his place since we would both be drinking. He had kissed my cheek in the car, and we had held hands, both enjoying the quiet on the short trip to the restaurant. I liked not having to fill the time with empty chatter. I had never been very good at small talk. Since we had sat down, though, conversation had flowed, and I was enjoying every moment with Jordan.

"I concur," he said, tasting his wine. "How we're supposed to get through seven courses, I'm not sure."

I indicated our plates. "I'm not sure we're supposed to finish everything they give us."

He shook his head. "Nope, too good."

He was right. The portions weren't huge, but I had noticed other people literally taking a bite and leaving the rest. Jordan and I cleared our plates. Spicy, shredded lamb and vegetable rolls. Ahi tuna with a drizzle of citrusy glaze on top of crispy noodles. Each course was delicious and the wine that accompanied it, heady.

I finished my pasta and sat back to enjoy the last of my wine. Jordan mimicked my position.

"Did I mention how lovely you look tonight?"

"Ah, no."

"How remiss of me. You are stunning, Sandy." He tilted his head. "You took your hair down." He lowered his voice. "Was that for me?"

I was shocked how husky my voice sounded. "Yes."

He eyed me over his wineglass. "Thank you."

How did he do that? Lovely, soft-spoken words that wrapped around me like a hug. Unspoken thoughts that promised more as the night went along. I found my gaze straying to his mouth. How had I never noticed his full lips before now? How soft they looked. Felt against mine.

How much I wanted to feel them again.

As if he knew what I was thinking, he smiled, his tongue touching his lower lip. I had to duck my head, feeling that odd sensation of needing to blush again.

Dammit.

"I was talking to Gina on Sunday."

I looked up. "How is she?"

"Good. Busy with the kids."

"You miss them."

"I do, but they're happy and Eric is doing really well with his new position. They're exactly where they should be." Then he inhaled deeply. "I talked to her about a decision I've made."

"Oh?"

"I'm going to sell my house."

"Where will you live?" I asked, my throat tight. Was he moving? I was shocked to realize how the thought of him leaving distressed me.

He frowned, then leaned over the table, offering me his hand. I slipped mine into his, and he squeezed my fingers. "To a condo—here in Toronto. I'm not going anywhere, Sandy. I wouldn't start something with you if I planned to disappear from your life."

My shoulders relaxed and I sighed. I hadn't even known how tightly I was holding myself until he spoke.

"Oh."

He squeezed my fingers again, not releasing my hand. "I would never do anything to cause you pain."

I nodded and reached for my wine. Our fingers remained entwined on the table.

"So, a condo?" I asked.

"It's time," he said. "I've been thinking about it for a while. The house is too big for only me. I don't use the pool much, and the gardens are getting overgrown. I need to downsize. The house needs a young family."

"Have you spoken to Bentley about it?"

"No."

"They still have a few units in Ridge Towers they kept aside. Maybe one of them would suit you."

"That's a good idea." Then he chuckled. "He'll grill me about it. You know that."

"Quite possibly. I think you can handle him."

His fingers flexed on mine. "I think you're right."

"You're not moving because of me, are you?"

He drained his wine and pursed his lips. "I'll be honest. Your presence in my life has factored into the decision a little."

"We're very early on in a relationship to make a drastic change like that, Jordan."

"I've been thinking of this for a while now. Gina brought it up when she was here again at Christmas, and I've been thinking about it more and more." He sat back. "I have every confidence in our fledgling relationship, Sandy. The bottom line is I don't want to make love to you in a place you shared with Max or one I shared with Anna."

His words astounded me. To him, it was a given. Our relationship would move forward and become intimate. We would become a couple.

"Wouldn't a hotel be cheaper?" I asked weakly. "A lot less stuff to move."

He threw back his head in laughter. "Hotels are fun too, but I want a place we can be together and create our own memories." He held up his hand before I could respond. "I'm not trying to put pressure on you, or us, here. It's simply my time for a fresh start. But if you're in my life, it makes it an even better decision."

I blinked. Then again. I sipped the last of my wine. I looked down where our fingers were still clasped together. I wasn't worried about Jordan pressuring me, and given what a thoughtful man he was, it shouldn't surprise me he had thought about our future. He would consider all factors in such a major decision.

"All right, then."

"Good. Glad we cleared the air." He winked. "I told Gina we'd been on a date."

"How did she take it?"

He smiled. "She was shocked I'd waited as long as I did to ask you. Apparently, Sandy, I talk about you a lot."

I had no response to that statement. "Oh."

"She is fine with it, by the way. She just wants me to be happy."

"And I make you happy?"

He smiled, and once again, I felt the reassuring press of his fingers. "You do."

I was surprised at the words I uttered.

"You make me happy too, Jordan."

T wo hours later, we headed to the car. Neither of us was exactly drunk, but we weren't sober either. The food was wonderful, the wine delicious, and the courses more decadent as the night progressed. The final pairing of a Canadian ice wine with a rich, thick brownie dipped in the darkest of chocolate was addictive. We enjoyed the ice wine so much, Jordan announced we were going to go to the winery and purchase some this weekend. I had no problem with his decision.

He nodded, his voice firm. "It can count as one of the dates."

I was sure I giggled, but I must have been mistaken. I never giggled.

Once in the car, Jordan slipped his arm around me, holding me close to his side. The driver told us a concert had just let out and the traffic was heavier than usual this time of night. Jordan waved him off.

"Not a problem."

The driver chuckled and raised the partition. I frowned.

"Why did he do that?"

"Maybe because he knew I was going to do this," Jordan's voice was pitched low. He slipped his hand under my chin, turning my face to his. Then his lips—those full, soft lips—were on mine.

He kissed me gently, our mouths moving together seamlessly. He slanted his head, cupping the back of my neck and bringing me closer. The kiss deepened. His tongue twisted with mine, stroking and tasting.

Chocolate. Cinnamon. Jordan.

The combination was heady, and I wanted more of it. I wrapped my hands around his neck and pulled him closer, letting him lead. The effect of the earlier alcohol was nothing compared to how drunk I was on his caresses. Endlessly, we kissed, sharing touches and whispered words of wonder. He discovered the spot behind my ear that drove me crazy. I found that he loved the feel of my tongue on his neck.

We both determined we lost track of time, and when the car stopped. I realized we'd been making out like teenagers for thirty minutes. We broke apart, both of us breathing hard. Jordan straightened his tie, shook his head to clear it, and slipped from the car, offering me his hand. He walked me to my door, waiting as I unlocked it. I felt the heat of him behind me, caught a whiff of his sexy cologne that was now soaked into my clothing from being pressed against him. His breath drifted across my neck, making me shiver. My fingers shook as I tried to get the key into the lock, and with a low chuckle, he covered my hand with his and steadied it.

He followed me inside, shutting the door. His gaze was warm, his smile indulgent. He traced one finger down my cheek, stopping at my mouth. Lazily, he ran his finger along my bottom lip.

"You are sweet. Addictive." He lifted his eyebrow. "Dangerous."

"I could say the same."

He leaned down and kissed me. The lightest brush of his mouth on mine. "Then I guess it's a good thing we're together."

I barely recognized my voice. "I guess so."

He stepped away. "It amazes me how difficult it is to walk away from you already."

I swallowed. "I'll see you tomorrow. Text me when you get home."

He lifted my hand and kissed it. "Goodnight."

EIGHT

JORDAN

Bentley and Aiden glanced at each other after I explained what I was interested in.

"How big a condo unit do you want, Jordan?" Bentley asked.

"I was thinking a two-bedroom. I can use the spare room as an office and a guest room for when my daughter visits."

He nodded, concentrating on the screen in front of him. "We have three left. Plus a three-bedroom. It's on the top floor, great views, and is actually the best value for money, square-foot wise."

"I'm trying to downsize, Bentley. The three-bedrooms are over twenty-two-hundred square feet."

Aiden spoke up. "Some, like Maddox's, are larger. The one we have is in building B and was made a little smaller because the person who shares that part wanted a larger unit. The three- bedroom is just under two-thousand square feet."

I pursed my lips.

"Why don't you look at both and decide?" Bentley offered. "You may not like either, and if that's the case, no pressure."

Aiden chuckled. "They're one of the most well-made condos around, and the management is top-notch."

I laughed along with them. "I'd heard that."

BAM only built the best. There was no cutting corners with them —ever. This project had been a massive undertaking for them, and I was proud to have been associated with it.

"If you don't like them, Jordan, what about the new project? The fifty-five-plus compound we're building?"

"Those won't be ready for a while, and I want to move fairly quickly, Bentley. I like the idea of the individual houses, but it's also a little out of town while I'm still working. Maybe once I think of retirement."

Bentley regarded me for a moment, his intense blue eyes meeting mine steadily. "First off, I hope that's a long way off, Jordan. Second, we plan on holding back a few places for lease only. There are always those who prefer not to own, so we cater to those individuals as well. If you decided you wanted one of those places, you could buy direct from us."

I smiled. "Knowing you, Bentley, by the time I retire, you'll have a dozen other places I can pick from. But for now, I would like to see the units you have at Ridge Towers."

"I'll take you there today myself. Maddox will come with us since he has all the numbers and can answer any of your questions."

Aiden piped up. "I think I'll join you."

I waved my hand. "Not necessary. I know you're busy."

"I insist."

I stood, knowing Bentley wouldn't move on this. "All right."

"Two o'clock."

"Fine. I'll meet you there."

I almost made it to the door when he asked.

"Will Sandy be joining us?"

Such an innocent question. Asked casually as if it was an afterthought, when I knew it was anything but.

I glanced over my shoulder. "I hadn't asked her, but perhaps I will. She can offer me an objective opinion."

Bentley nodded. "That's a good idea."

Aiden leaned back in his chair, grinning like a loon. I left the office before I started to laugh.

Sandy was right—overgrown, curious children. All of them.

Sandy and I walked around the two units, opening cupboards, listening as Reid, who'd found out about the trip and insisted on joining us, blathered on about the technical wonders he'd added.

As part of the company, I had watched these towers being built. Attended design meetings and looked over the blueprints many times. Toured the buildings once they were complete. But looking at the units as a prospective buyer was a different experience.

I opened the patio door and stepped onto the balcony, staring at the vista in front of me. This unit was on the side of the building that overlooked the water. I liked that, plus the fact that there was a small marina being added. I could walk to my boat. The drive into the office would take a little longer, but given the early hours I usually went in, it would be worth it for the ease of access to my boat.

Sandy stepped out beside me, laying her hands on the rail. "It's surprisingly quiet."

"They've designed this very well." I swept my gaze over the land-scape. The wooded area with a trail leading down to the water. The outside pool and tennis court. The feel of a small resort while still being at home. "It's amazing."

"Is it for you, though?"

"It would be a big change. I need to think it over carefully." I glanced at her out of the corner of my eye. "How vigilantly are we being watched?"

She peeked over her shoulder, then chuckled and turned back. "Desperately trying to act casual and failing."

"I can't believe they're all here."

"They're trying to act as if all the partners show off units all the time." She snorted softly. "As if."

"What are they expecting?"

"I have no idea. I think they wanted to see us together. See how we act?"

"I imagine they're pretty disappointed." I snickered. Sandy and I had acted as if we were in the office, discussing details of the units in a businesslike manner, standing apart, not touching.

She laughed softly. "Serves them right."

"Do you think they know what I really want to do is hold your hand?" I asked quietly. "Pull you down on that bed in the master bedroom and lie there with you so I would know how it felt to open my eyes in the morning and not only see that view but see it with you beside me? Kiss you in the kitchen and see how you feel pressed against that imported marble?"

Her breath caught, but she didn't turn her head. "Jordan…"

I slid my hand along the rail, covering hers. "Can you see yourself here, Sandy? Coming for dinner, spending time with me?"

For a moment, we stared at the view. Listened to the muted sound of laughter coming from down below.

Finally, she turned her head and met my eyes. "I would come and spend time with you anywhere, Jordan. If you're asking if I like this place, then the answer is yes. If you're asking if maybe one day, I would do those things you just described—" she let out a quivering sigh "—the answer is yes. One day I would."

Then she turned, kissed my cheek, and walked back inside.

SANDY

Back at the office, I had trouble concentrating. It was an odd feeling for me. Usually, I was able to turn off my thoughts about anything but the office and only focus on the task at hand.

But not since returning from the condo visit. When I stepped back into the condo, leaving Jordan outside, I felt the stares of all the partners. Jordan followed me, standing close, his hand settling into the small of my back.

"I think I've seen enough. I need to do some thinking now."

I traveled back to the office with Jordan, but he remained quiet, other than thanking me for coming with him. When we arrived at the office, he received a message on his phone.

"I have a real estate agent coming over tonight to look at the house. She was recommended by Bentley."

"All right."

"May I call you once she leaves?"

I slipped my hand into his. "Yes."

Before the doors opened, he bent down and kissed me on the cheek.

"Thank you."

I still felt the warmth of his lips.

Jordan sat with the boys, leaving Bentley's office with a sheaf of papers. He winked at me as he went by, and I smiled as I dealt with one of the many people Bentley needed to call back. His impromptu outing had caused some glitches in his schedule, but I knew I would smooth it all out quickly for him. He would have to work late today—a rare occurrence now. It used to be he was the first in the office and the last to go, but once Emmy became part of his life, that changed. Since Addi was born, he rarely was in the office past six. He was always anxious to get home to his girls.

I shook my head and focused my attention on the work in front of me. The rest of the afternoon sped by, and I left the office with Bentley, who insisted on Frank driving me home. In the car, he was quiet, staring out the window.

The car pulled up in front of my house, but before I could get out, Bentley spoke.

"Sandy."

I turned to him, my hand on the door handle.

"All kidding aside, you know we want what is best for you, right?"

"I know," I assured him.

"Jordan seems very attentive."

"He is." I let go of the handle and turned to him. "This is still very new. I don't know if it will go anywhere. I don't know if I'm ready for it to go anywhere. But I do know this. Jordan makes me smile. He makes me feel lighter. Less alone. I feel more like Sandy when I'm with him, if that makes any sense."

"It does. I'm more me with Emmy than I am with anyone else."

I squeezed his hand. "Yes."

"He watches you. Today, I saw how important your opinion was to him. How it would factor in his decision. I think his feelings already run deep."

"I know. He's been upfront with me."

"How do you feel about that?"

I sighed, contemplating his words for a moment. "Happy. Anxious. Safe. Worried. Scared. Incredulous."

"That's a lot of feelings."

"That's called being a woman, Bentley."

He leaned forward, gathering my hands in his. "You deserve to be happy, Sandy. You know that, right?"

"I know."

"Max loved you, and he hated the thought of you being alone. He would want you to be happy and cared for." His blue eyes were intense as he stared at me. "I know what alone is like, Sandy. You have so much to give. So much love. You deserve to have that given back to you."

I blinked at the sudden moisture in my eyes. "Is that your way of giving me your blessing?"

He smiled. "That's my way of saying grab happiness, Sandy. Look forward, not behind you."

"Sometimes easier said than done."

"Your past made you the woman you are. Let the future benefit from that."

I swallowed. "At times, I worry it's too soon."

"What you and Max shared was special and rare. But with a heart as big as yours, you can love again." Bentley tilted his head. "Loving again isn't a betrayal to Max, Sandy. It's a tribute. It shows how well he loved you."

"When did you get so smart?" I asked.

He bent close and kissed my cheek. "I learned from you."

I sat at my table, staring into the glass of wine I had poured. I pushed away my plate, the sandwich I had made not tempting me at all. But I didn't feel like cooking. Or eating.

I picked up the wine and headed toward the living room. My doorbell echoing in the emptiness of the house startled me. I looked at the screen of my phone, surprised, but pleased, to see Jordan on my doorstep.

I opened the door, smiling. "Hello. I didn't expect to see you tonight."

He hesitated. "Is it all right that I came over? I know I said I would call—"

I cut him off with a wave of my hand. "Of course. Come in."

He strode in, stopping to kiss my cheek, his lips brushing my skin, leaving a trail of warmth.

I took his coat, got him a glass of wine, and sat next to him on the sofa. "Did you have dinner?" I asked.

"I had a sandwich."

I laughed. "Me too." I indicated the file in his hand. "What's that?"

"This is what I came here to talk about." He faced me fully on the sofa. "I need your unbiased advice, Sandy."

I tilted my head to the side. "I'm not sure how unbiased I can be about you anymore, Jordan," I confessed.

He smiled and closed the space between us to drop a kiss on my mouth. "I like hearing that, but I think you can be in this case."

I squared my shoulders. "Okay, hit me."

He opened the file and spread out the documents. "This is the asking price the real estate agent has suggested."

I read the large number. "Given the market, that seems right."

He chuckled. "I bought the house for less than two hundred grand thirty years ago. I never imagined it would be valued at over ten times that price one day."

"Toronto is hot. And it's a large house with a yard in a great neighborhood. It's hardly surprising."

He set another document on top. "This is the price Bentley gave me for the condo."

I glanced at the amount, noting he had chosen the larger one with three bedrooms. It had been my favorite as well. "That's in line with what he gave to Maddox and Reid."

"But they're partners, Sandy. I'm not a partner. This is well below market value."

"Bentley believes in rewarding staff, Jordan. To him, you are as valuable as Reid and Maddox. As any of his staff." I smiled as I teased him. "If you're worried about Bentley's bottom line, I assure you he made millions on this project. And the way Maddox structured and invested the holdings, he'll make many more."

He chuckled, then rested his chin on his hand as he studied the papers. "He also told me I could have the condo whenever I wanted it if I decided to go ahead with this. The agent said she would help me thin out the house and put things in storage if needed." He was silent for a moment. "One signature—one stroke on a pen, and my entire life as I know it will change."

"Are you ready for that?" I asked.

He pushed at the papers with his finger. Back and forth, he moved them in a repeated restless pattern.

"There's no smoking gun here, Jordan. You don't have to decide tonight, or even this week. Maybe you should talk to your kids about it. Look at the condo again."

He met my gaze. "That's the odd thing. I'm not conflicted or worried. I really liked the condo, and the thought of not having to deal with all the outside stuff and being alone in the house, filled with nothing but recollections of what my life was like before, is actually a relief. I want to sign the papers. Move ahead."

"And that worries you."

One corner of his mouth lifted in a lopsided grin. "Yes. It's not like me. I'm usually a very methodical decision-maker."

"Perhaps there's another way to think of this then, Jordan."

"Tell me."

"Maybe you had already thought it through. You told me when

Gina brought it up two years ago, you weren't ready. That when Gina questioned you again at Christmas, you had already begun to change your mind. You said you've been thinking about it ever since. As for the condo, they say you know if the place is right for you ten seconds after you walk in the door."

He stared at the documents, deep in thought. He turned his head, a smile ghosting his lips. "You are a very clever woman, Sandy Preston."

I laughed. "I try." Then I became serious. "Do what it is you want to do—for *you*, Jordan. Nobody else." I exhaled. "Don't factor me into your decision."

"Are you breaking up with me already?" he asked lightly, although his eyes were worried.

"No, but we're still so new. Make this decision as if this happened two weeks ago, not now. Can you do that?"

"It would still be the same."

"Then do it."

He relaxed back into the sofa, and I handed him the glass of wine. He sipped it.

"Have you ever thought of selling?" he asked.

I glanced around the room, its familiarity comforting and safe. "Not yet," I admitted. "One day, maybe."

"Did you and Max buy this together?"

"No, actually, he bought it after his divorce. I didn't meet him for almost ten years afterward. He told me we could move, but I liked the character of the house and he was settled here, and I saw no point in doing so. He'd never shared it with his wife, so there were no memories to compete with. He gave me free rein, and I decorated it to suit us. It was rather, ah, masculine when I moved in. And he'd never touched the kids' rooms, so they were a little dated."

"Did you ever meet his first wife?"

I nodded. "We got on quite well. She was a little shocked at the age difference, as most people were, but she was cordial. We were all adults." She winked. "Some of them more adult-y than I was."

Jordan laughed.

"Our plan had always been to give this place to Colin. When I'm ready to move, I'll do that."

"That's very generous."

I shrugged. "He's the light of my life. I adore him, and he works very hard. He refused to let us pay off his student loans, so a mort-gage-free home will help. I only hope one day he finds the right person to share it with."

"I'm going to use some of the money from the sale and set up college funds for my grandkids. Neither Gina or Warren will take any of my money otherwise, no matter how many times I have offered. This way, I can help in a roundabout manner." He took a sip of wine. "Not sure Warren will ever have a child, but I'll set aside the same amount in case."

"When will you tell your kids?"

"Right away. I want them to come and pick out anything they want from the house. I plan on donating a lot to charity and buying new furniture. Aside from some select items and personal things, I want a fresh start."

"You've really thought this through."

"I suppose I have."

"Congratulations." I raised my glass. "To new beginnings."

Jordan lifted his glass. "If I can be so bold—to shared new beginnings."

I touched my glass to his and tried not to blush.

This time, I failed.

NINE

SANDY

Jordan extended his hand, his expression one of indulgence. "Come aboard."

"It's a little, ah, choppier than the other night."

He chuckled. "Only because of the breeze. Perfect for a day on the boat."

I glanced at the sky. "You sure it won't storm?"

"Nope. These clouds will move away, and the sun will be out within the hour." He waggled his fingers. "Come on, Sandy. I got you."

I let him pull me onboard, still nervous but not wanting to tell him why. Storms made me stressed enough on dry land. Never mind being pitched about in a boat. I wasn't sure I could handle that.

He handed me the picnic basket I had packed earlier. "You store this below, and I'll get us going. The light is brighter toward Niagara."

"Okay."

I went down the few steps and figured out the layout of the small galley kitchen, storing away our lunch. I felt the boat moving and grabbed the thermal carafe of coffee I had brought with me. Jordan was behind the wheel, guiding the boat from the marina. He held out his arm, and I slipped in front of him, his chest pressed to my back.

"I thought you had sails."

"I do. I use the engine to get to open water or when there's no wind. I'll unfurl the sail in a while."

"It's pretty out here."

"It is. I love being on the water." He dropped his mouth to my ear. "I love being out here with you, my darling."

My heart clenched at his endearment. I lifted my head, meeting his gaze. He lowered his, kissing me, his lips moving with mine.

Jordan Hayes could kiss. If it were an art form, he would be a master. Every time our mouths met, I never wanted it to end.

He lifted his head and smiled, drawing his fingers down my cheek. "That will have to hold me until we clear the marina. I don't want to run into another boat."

"Oh."

He kept one hand on the wheel, wrapping his other arm around my waist. "But you stay right where you are. I like you here."

I snuggled closer, feeling the way his arm tightened. I had to admit, I liked it right there as well.

The sun burst from behind the cloud, its rays skittering across the waves, reflecting on the boat. I lifted my face to its warmth, enjoying the feel of it and the breeze that blew around us. The sail snapped and filled, stretched tight as the boat raced through the water, smooth and steady. Jordan leaned back, looking satisfied. "We'll be there in about an hour. I thought we'd tie up at the marina, rent a couple of bikes, hit those wineries we got the names of. Both of them are only about a ten-minute ride from the marina. We can go look anywhere else you want to, then we can head back to the boat, find a cove, and throw down the anchor. Have lunch and enjoy the sun before we head back."

I was touched by his planning. "Sounds lovely."

Soon, we docked in the marina, and once again, I marveled at the ease he had handling his boat. He moored us to the dock, then jumped onto the wooden planks, extending his hand and pulling me up with him. He tucked me into his side.

"Let's go find an adventure, my darling."

I reached up and cupped his face, kissing him. He was smiling when I pulled back.

"What?"

"That's the first time you've kissed *me*."

"Maybe I was just getting warmed up."

His green eyes glowed, and he kissed the end of my nose. He tugged his sunglasses down, then did the same to mine. "Good to know."

I hugged his arm. "Let's go."

We wandered to the bike shop, setting out using the directions they gave us. In the end, we visited three wineries, filling the large baskets on the bikes with several bottles. We'd had a few samples, argued playfully over our favorites, then bought them all. We stopped at a small roadside shop selling local honey and preserves and added a few jars to the basket as well.

We detoured back to the boat, unloading the wine, then we headed back to drop off the bikes. We discovered an outdoor market and spent some time meandering among the booths. I bought a few local crafts that caught my eye, and Jordan picked up a new windbreaker one shop was selling. He slipped it on, pulling up the zipper, and waited for my approval. I pursed my lips, then shook my head. "The navy one. The white makes you look washed out."

"Your lady knows you well," the shopkeeper stated. "She's right."

Jordan tried on the navy jacket, and I gave my approval. "Perfect."

He flipped through the rack and held up a matching jacket in a smaller size. "Try this on."

Frowning, I slid my arms in and let him tug up the zipper. He stood back and nodded. "Yes."

He turned to the owner. "I'll take both."

"I don't need a windbreaker, Jordan. Where on earth will I wear it?"

He smiled and leaned down to brush his mouth against mine. "On the boat, with me."

"Oh."

Holding hands, we strolled the busy streets, stopping to look in windows. Jordan pointed out the Christmas store, and we went inside, marveling at all the Christmas items and displays.

"Makes me want to start decorating," I mused.

Jordan chuckled. "A bit early."

"I suppose."

He kissed the end of my nose playfully. "I'll bring you back in the fall, and you can pick a bunch of things."

"Promise?"

He wound his arm around my waist, pulling me close. He dropped a kiss to my mouth. "Promise," he breathed against my lips, then pulled back, smiling.

I was going to ask why he was smiling so hard, then realized the reason myself. He expected us to still be together in the fall.

I had to admit, the thought of that made me smile as well.

Finally, we went back to the boat. "I'm starving," Jordan groaned.

"We ate those treats we got at the bakery."

The sticky buns had beckoned from the window, the aroma enticing. We went inside and bought two, eating them as we walked, then licking our fingers to get rid of the stickiness.

"That barely tided me over."

"Do you want to eat now?"

"No. I know a great little cove we can pull into and have lunch. I'll have us there in ten minutes."

"Okay, I'll get lunch ready."

Jordan sat back, patting his stomach. "Ah, much better."

I laughed, plucking a piece of melon from the container and popping it into my mouth. "I think you gave Aiden a run for his money today."

"I built up an appetite with the bike riding and all that walking."

"We got some great things, though."

He grinned, touching the sleeve of my windbreaker. "Like our matching jackets."

I laughed. "Our boat uniforms."

He joined in my amusement. "Yes."

We had spread out a blanket on the deck and Jordan added a

couple of pillows from below. With the sun still out and the breeze from the water, it was lovely. The little cove was deserted, the water calm, and it felt as if we were the only two people around. It was a relaxing way to pass the afternoon, and I was beginning to understand Jordan's love of being on the water.

"Do you ever stay overnight on the boat?"

"On occasion. It's not very big, but for a weekend, it's fine." He drew his legs up to his chest, wrapping his arms around his knees. "I'd love to rent a houseboat and travel through the Thousand Islands and into Quebec. Spend weeks on the water, just drifting and exploring."

"You can do that?"

"Oh yes. I went on a short trip once and enjoyed it. Some of them are quite luxurious. Well-equipped kitchens, sun decks you can sit on and enjoy the evenings. Spacious bedrooms." He smiled. "It's always been a dream of mine to do a trip on my own."

"Sounds wonderful."

He cocked his head, studying me. "Would that interest you, Sandy? Or is that too casual a vacation for you?"

"Casual? Aren't vacations supposed to be casual?"

He stretched out his legs, leaning back on his hands. "I suppose. To me, the houseboat represents peace. Days spent in the sun wearing my swim trunks. Maybe a T-shirt and shorts. Casual and easy. The fanciest thing I'd bring with me would be a pair of Dockers and a polo shirt to have dinner onshore on occasion."

I stared at him, my imagination going wild. I had seen Jordan bare-chested once. He'd been down in the gym with Aiden, Van, and Maddox, playing basketball. They were all laughing and talking smack, sweating with their shirts off. I was used to seeing the boys bare-chested, but it was Jordan who had drawn my eye. He had a muscular chest, and it was obvious from the way his muscles rippled he still worked out and took good care of himself. His shorts had hung low on his hips, showing off his still flat stomach, and he stood with his hands on his hips as he jeered at Maddox. His biceps bunched as he leaned forward, ready to defend the net.

He had looked so sexy, I had to step back and clear my head before letting them know I was there. I made sure not to look in his direction when I reentered the gym and told Aiden that Bentley needed him right away.

The thought of him wandering a boat in his swimsuit made my temperature rise.

Jordan frowned. "Sandy?"

I blinked. "Sorry?"

"I lost you for a moment."

"Oh, ah, I was thinking about your question. I imagine an extended stay on a houseboat would be quite delightful." I improvised.

"Well then, I suppose we'll have to discuss that at a later date."

"Oh, um, yes."

"What about you?" he asked, sliding a piece of melon into his mouth and chewing. "What kind of vacation do you like?"

I shrugged. "I love exploring places. England, Scotland, other countries in Europe. But I also love staying closer to home. I love the idea of jetting off for a weekend. Somewhere different but easy to get to. We did that a few times, and I loved it. Just a break away somewhere different."

"Not for a while, though?" he guessed.

"No. Max found traveling very taxing. I went away on occasion for a weekend, but not for years. The last one I planned got canceled when he had a bad episode. I never planned another."

"Where were you supposed to go?"

I sighed as I remembered. "Boston. With Colin. We were going to eat seafood, go to the MFA—there was a collection of Renoirs on loan I wanted to see. We were going to tour Salem, walk on Boston Commons, and see the harbor. Colin wanted to go to a baseball game in Fenway Park." I lifted one shoulder. "One day, I will."

"I'm certain you will," he murmured.

We fell into a comfortable silence, simply enjoying the quiet. It was remarkable that, with Jordan, the quiet didn't bother me the way it did when I was alone. With him sitting beside me, it was calming and peaceful.

I broke off a chunk of the dark chocolate we had picked up at the market and offered him a piece. I let it melt on my tongue and shut my eyes, enjoying the decadent, rich flavor. "This is amazing."

"Yes, it is."

I opened my eyes, flushing when I realized although he'd taken and eaten a piece of chocolate, he was staring at me.

I felt the heat in my cheeks. "Dammit, Jordan Hayes," I muttered. "I keep blushing like a schoolgirl. Stop it."

He chuckled. "I like making you blush. It's unusual for you."

I huffed out an exasperated noise. "Because, until you, it never happened."

He slid closer so our knees were touching. He drifted his fingers along my cheek. "I like it even better now."

Our gazes locked, the silence between us no longer peaceful. It bubbled and shimmered with longing. Jordan's gaze dropped to my mouth, and he ran his tongue along his bottom lip. I tracked the sensuous gesture, my breathing picking up.

"If I come closer to kiss you, are you going to let me?"

"Yes," I breathed out with no hesitation.

He pushed closer, lifting my legs on top of his so they rested over his hips. He tugged my waist, drawing me close until we were nose to nose, hardly any space between us. I felt his warmth, the firmness of his body as he leaned into me. The breeze lifted his thick hair, and I ran my fingers through it, settling my arm around his neck and playing with the nape of his neck. He shivered.

"I love it when you touch me, Sandy."

I recalled his delight from earlier when I had taken the initiative and kissed him. I closed the final inches between us and pressed my mouth to his. His reaction was immediate. He wrapped his arms around me, yanking me tight to his chest, practically pulling me onto his lap. He buried his hands in my hair, slanting his mouth and taking control of the kiss. This wasn't like our other kisses. There were no soft, languid movements. This was passion, heat, and possession. Sensations I hadn't experienced for years. His tongue delved, stroking, seeking, exploring. He tasted of the chocolate we'd shared. Melon. Wine. Jordan. It was a heady combination.

I gasped in his mouth as he slipped his hands under the loose cotton shirt I wore. His long fingers traced my spine, sending shards of pleasure through my body. I felt him, hard between us, his desire evident.

I groaned low in my throat as he dragged his mouth to my ear, teasing the spot behind it.

"Sandy," he whispered. "God, I want you."

I whimpered, grasping his shirt with one hand as I clutched his neck with the other. He trailed his mouth down my neck, tasting my skin with his tongue. He nudged my collar out of the way, burying his face between my breasts. The feel of his hands moving over my rib cage, sliding up, his thumbs strumming over my hardened nipples was intense. Addictive.

Making me want more.

Until the sound of another boat entering the cove and blowing its horn broke us apart. We were both breathing hard, our eyes locked in a haze of desire. Jordan's cheeks were flushed, his hair in disarray from my hands. My shirt was rumpled, and I knew my hair looked as if I had stood in a wind tunnel. My mouth was swollen and so was Jordan's. His was red and wet from my tongue, and I wanted it back on mine. I knew if the boat hadn't shown up, we would have ended up naked and writhing on the deck of the boat, the sun and breeze witness to our passion.

Then the hilarity of the moment hit me, and I giggled. I clapped a hand over my mouth, but I couldn't stop. Jordan's mouth quirked, and he began to laugh.

"Damn it," he cursed. "Caught like a seventeen-year-old on my parents' sofa."

I kept laughing. Jordan caught me in his arms, and I leaned on his shoulder, the entire situation too ludicrous not to enjoy. He laughed with me, muttering about better planning. Once I got myself under control, I sat up, meeting his gaze. He looked at me with such tenderness, my heart skipped a beat.

"We should head back," he said, stroking my cheek.

I captured his hand. "Thank you for today, Jordan. It was perfect."

I meant what I said. The boat arrived before we had crossed a line we couldn't back away from. I was certain we would both know when the time was right to cross that boundary. After today, I certainly looked forward to it, but today was not that day, and we were both aware of it.

He smiled and kissed me fast. "Yes, it was, my darling. Yes, it was."

TEN

The next few days were a whirlwind.

With Van moving in to the new space, he was in and out of the office, overseeing his crews, and still working on various projects. Jordan helped him when he could, so he was often out of the building as well. Add in the fact that Jordan was preparing his house for sale, and he was a busy man. He made sure to keep in contact, though. I enjoyed his texts and phone calls on the days I didn't see him.

The final construction was completed on the day care in the office building, and Bentley proudly brought Addi with him to work in order to show her what he had created for her.

I followed him around as he held her close, pointing out all the fun things in the nursery, talking about how she would have friends here and be near to him. He was obviously excited about her being in the building.

He lifted her in the air. "Daddy will be right down the hall and can come visit anytime. So will Mommy. Won't that be great?"

She blinked at him, her eyes wide in her face. Before I could warn him, she opened her mouth and puked down the front of his expensive suit.

He turned his head to me, his expression all at once confused, uncertain, and slightly disturbed.

"I think she just ate," I murmured.

"Emmy mentioned that," he confirmed. "I forgot."

He handed her to me as he slipped off his jacket, then cradled her back in his arms, cooing down at her, using his handkerchief to wipe her face. I enjoyed seeing his softer side. He showed it to very few people, but his wife and daughter saw it the most.

"You have a fresh suit in the closet."

"Good thing."

I chuckled. "Yes, it is."

He rocked Addi, nodding in satisfaction at the large room. With Maddox's wife, Dee, pregnant, plus Aiden and Cami trying, I knew he was looking forward to the day the room was filled with BAM babies. I knew he already planned on expanding the day care for other staff members, but it required some reconfiguring of the building. He would sort it out—of that, I had no doubt.

He glanced up. "Have you spoken to Jordan?"

I smiled. "Of course. He is almost ready to put the house up for sale. He says he can't believe the difference a few days have made."

Bentley grinned. "That's what I hire the best for. Many hands make light work."

Bentley had sent a team over to Jordan's house, along with one of the decorators. They had moved, packed, and staged his house, and it would be going up for sale by the weekend. His unneeded possessions had been moved to one of the many warehouses BAM owned, so Jordan could take his time going through the items. Jordan had worked from home the past few days while it was being done, and I had to admit, I missed seeing him in the office. But we were having dinner tonight, and I was looking forward to it. I was cooking dinner at my place so Jordan could just relax.

"It's happening so fast."

Bentley cocked his head, his voice soft. "The sale of his house, or something else, Sandy?"

I smiled ruefully and took Addi from his arms, wanting to feel her warmth.

"His house, his new place, and yes, I suppose the relationship we're in."

Bentley shrugged, patting at the damp spot on his tie with his handkerchief. "The house was easy. Jordan was ready, the house only needed the minimum of staging, and the crew is efficient." He gave up on his tie, tugging it over his neck and stuffing it in his pocket. "The condo was simple. Paperwork is something Jordan excels at." He smirked. "He's letting Liv help decorate it once she's back from her honeymoon next month, so again—simple. I have a feeling his house will go quickly, and he can move forward, which brings us to the last point—your relationship."

"A very succinct overview."

He rolled his eyes. "That's what *I* excel at. Frankly, I was worried about you and Jordan having a relationship, but both of you look happier than I've seen you in a long time. You complement each other, and it's good to see you smile. I know it's scary—all relationships are scary—but you have a lot to offer each other, and I'm enjoying watching him woo you."

"Is that a fact?"

Reid stepped into the room. "We're *all* enjoying that."

I glared at him. "I don't think anyone asked for your opinion, young man."

Reid laughed, not at all put out by my tone. "Bent, Maddox is looking for you. He needs some stuff signed."

Bentley took Addi from me and headed to the door. "I'll leave you to it, then."

Reid turned to me, a wide smile firmly in place. "We've all noticed, Sandy."

"Noticed what, exactly?"

"The little bunches of flowers. The small boxes of chocolate that appear on your desk. The fact that you actually leave the building for lunch—at the same time Jordan does, by the way. And that funny little grin you sport when he sends you a text."

"How do you know it's Jordan sending me a text?"

Reid leaned closer, his eyes dancing. "He's the only person I know who makes you blush or smile that way."

I crossed my arms. My boys were far too observant.

Reid mimicked my action. "Not to mention the way your eyes

follow him when he walks away." He winked, his lips quirking. "I think you like his butt."

I gaped at him. "Reid Matthews!"

He bent to kiss my cheek, still smiling. "You once told me to grab happiness, Sandy. Take your own advice."

"Go back to your office and do some work. I am the one to give advice around here." I pushed him out the door. "And I do not stare at his...*butt,*" I added.

"Whatever," he called over his shoulder.

I watched him disappear around the corner, then began to chuckle.

I did stare—it was a nice butt. But for Reid to have noticed meant I needed to be more careful.

I couldn't let the boys have one up on me.

That simply wouldn't do.

The doorbell rang about seven. I finished stirring the pot and replaced the lid. I peeked in the oven, and satisfied, I hurried to the front door, opening it with a smile.

Jordan stood on my front porch, returning my smile. In one hand was a large bunch of lilies—my second favorite flower—and in the other, a bottle of wine.

He grinned at me, indicating my porch door with a tilt of his head. "The door squeaks. Needs some oil."

I winked. "No one can ever sneak in without me hearing them."

"Ah, good plan."

I waved him in, and he stepped past me, his woodsy scent filling the hall. I shut the door and turned to him. "Hello, stranger."

He set the wine on the table, holding out the flowers. I took the bouquet, inhaling the spicy fragrance of the lilies. I lifted my eyes to meet Jordan's gaze. His green eyes were soft, gentle, and filled with warmth.

"It feels like years since I saw you," he confessed.

"It's been four days."

He moved closer, sliding his arm around my waist. "Like I said, years."

He tugged me close and I wrapped my arms around his neck, the plastic encasing the flowers crinkling in protest. He lowered his head and I met him eagerly, his mouth hovering over mine.

"Hello, my darling."

Our lips touched, and the world ceased to exist. He gathered me close, the heat of his body soaking into mine. Our mouths moved together, sliding and tasting, refamiliarizing themselves with each other. His tongue stole in, caressing and light, then going deeper, his arms cinching me tighter. I cupped the back of his head, swimming in the sensations his touch brought out in me.

I had missed him—more than I realized. The hole, the feeling of emptiness closed up, and I felt alive and rejuvenated.

He explored me, his hands spread wide across my back, his mouth never ceasing its wicked possession. I clutched him close, never wanting this moment to end. I was lost to him. His taste, his feel, the safety I felt in his embrace.

Until reality exploded, and Colin walked in.

"Whoa—What the...?"

Jordan and I broke apart, both of us startled and gasping for air.

So much for not sneaking in. Neither of us had heard the porch door.

I stared at Colin, struck dumb. He looked between Jordan and me, an odd expression on his face. He lifted his hand and ran it through his hair, then began to chuckle.

"Nan, seriously. Making out in the front hall?"

I cleared my throat, totally flummoxed. "Ah, Colin, I wasn't expecting you."

He smirked. "Obviously. I assume it slipped your mind it was the second Thursday of the month?"

Oh no—it had slipped my mind totally. Colin always came for dinner the second Thursday of the month.

He began to laugh, not at all upset or even worried about the man standing beside me, with his arm around me, protective and wary.

Colin stuck out his hand. "Hello, Jordan." His lips twitched. "Nice to see you again. Unexpected, but nice."

For a moment, I was confused, then remembered Colin had seen Jordan in the office several times.

Jordan extended his hand. "Colin."

They shook hands, one bemused and smiling, the other cordial but tense. Colin spoke up.

"I assume you're joining us for dinner?"

Jordan glanced at me, and I lifted one shoulder. "Yes, he is," I stated.

Colin chuckled. "Teasing. How about we reschedule? I'll call you tomorrow."

I shook my head. "No, stay. You can have dinner with us." I drew in a long breath of air for bravery. "Get to know Jordan."

Colin smiled widely. "I'd like that."

I picked up the bottle of wine. "I'm going to check on dinner."

Colin headed toward the living room. "I'll get us drinks." He clapped his hands. "This is gonna be fun."

I met Jordan's amused gaze and mouthed, "Sorry."

He shook his head and pressed a kiss to my forehead. "He took that well," he muttered.

"I forgot," I whispered. "I forgot about our standing date because of you—you befuddled my head!" I slapped his chest. "What are you doing to me, Jordan Hayes?"

He lifted my chin, his eyes twinkling. "Not what I want to be doing right now."

That odd giggle escaped my throat. Jordan grinned and kissed the end of my nose. "I'm looking forward to getting to know him a little. I know how much you adore him."

Colin appeared in the door.

"Hey, kids, the sooner we have dinner, the sooner I leave, and you can get back to, ah, doing what you were doing. Let's go!"

I threw him a look that should have had him writhing on the floor.

Instead, he grinned widely. "Come on, Jordan. I know Nan is sexy, but I have some great scotch I keep here I'm willing to share."

Jordan chuckled and squeezed my hand as he moved past me. I sighed as I headed to the kitchen.

This was going to be an interesting evening—not at all what I planned—but interesting, nonetheless.

ELEVEN

I sat back, sipping my wine, listening as the two men I adored got to know each other. When I'd walked into the room earlier, they had been standing by the fireplace, talking in low voices, looking serious. But when they saw me, they both smiled and seemed at ease. Every time I left the room, their conversation began again, and I wondered what exactly they were talking about. They certainly seemed to have a lot to say to each other.

At dinner, Colin was his usual chatty self, catching me up on all the things happening at the hospital and in his life. He was busy, happy, and seemingly quite comfortable with Jordan. We kept the conversation neutral, and the atmosphere was cheerful.

He finished his second helping of dinner and set down his cutlery.

"Awesome coq au vin. One of your best yet."

Jordan hummed his agreement as Colin picked up his wine.

"So how long have you two been an item?" he asked casually.

I cleared my throat. "Not long."

"You looked pretty friendly when I walked in the door." He winked. "And I've never known you to forget about me coming over."

I felt my cheeks flush, and Colin began to laugh.

"Nan, are you blushing?" He slapped the table as he chuckled. "Jordan Hayes, what kind of effect are you having on her?"

Jordan joined in his amusement. "A good one, I hope." He reached for my hand and squeezed my fingers.

"I asked Sandy out a few weeks ago, Colin. We get along very well."

"I noticed," Colin deadpanned.

"I know you were close to your grandfather, and I hope my relationship with Sandy doesn't upset you. But I'm very fond of her, and I think she is of me as well. Surely, you want her to be happy?"

Colin sat up straighter, all teasing gone. He regarded Jordan and me briefly. "I want nothing more than for her to be happy. I haven't seen her smile like this for a very long time, and if you're the cause, then you have my full blessing. Not that you need it," he added with a shrug. "You're both adults and can do with your lives whatever you choose."

"I would prefer to have your blessing," I said, meeting his eyes. He reminded me of Max—he had his eyes and the same tall, slim build. "I wasn't looking for a relationship, but…" I trailed off.

Colin shook his head. "No, you're too young. Gramps would have wanted you to be happy. That was always one of his biggest worries. He knew, just like I do, that you have too much love in you not to have someone to share it with. He and I talked a lot about what would happen once he was gone."

That surprised me. "I didn't know."

He smiled. "He didn't want you to. We talked about a lot of things."

Jordan interrupted us. "Your grandfather was a great man. I met him several times, and I liked him a lot. He was very kind when my wife passed."

Colin smiled. "That doesn't surprise me. He was a kind man to everyone. He loved my nan fiercely."

"I know."

"Will you care for her the same way?"

Jordan shook his head. "I can't. No one will ever love Sandy the way Max did. I'm not looking to compete with him, Colin. The same way Sandy will never replace my wife's spot. But we can love another person just as strongly, though in a different way. How I feel about Sandy doesn't take away the life I shared with my Anna. I believe my past helps me to be able to love another person because I know the joy that brings. The loneliness another person can dispel." He leaned forward, his gaze steady on Colin. "I think Sandy and I can build something special together."

"You seem to be moving fast."

Jordan laughed, sitting back. "At our age, we have a wealth of experience behind us. We don't need to play games or test the large dating pool. I like your *nan*, she likes me, and that is all we need to know. We don't have the luxury of years ahead of us. If we're happy, then we're grabbing it. Living life now. Case closed."

Colin was silent, mulling over what Jordan said. Jordan lifted his wine and sent a subtle wink my way, making me smile.

I picked up my wine. "How are all your *Tinder* dates going, by the way? Any interesting, ah, *hookups* lately, Colin?"

He began to laugh. "Point taken, Nan. You'll be happy to know I deleted the app. I met a new nurse at the hospital. She is quite—" he swallowed "—lovely. She reminds me of you, actually. We've had three dates, and I was thinking of bringing her to meet you." He grinned. "Maybe we can double one night."

I smiled, hiding my surprise. Colin had never brought anyone to meet me. "I would like that."

"Me too."

He stood, placing his napkin on the table. "I should go. I have a five-a.m. shift tomorrow."

"What about dessert?"

He shook his head. "I've interrupted long enough." He reached across the table and shook Jordan's hand. "It's been a real pleasure. I hope to see more of you."

"You as well."

Colin winked. "You will."

I walked him to the door, and he turned to hug me. "I like him, Nan."

"I do too."

"I meant what I said. Be happy."

"I'm trying."

He pressed a kiss to my cheek. "Keep trying, Nan. I like seeing you this way."

"I'm sorry I forgot."

He shook his head. "That is the best part of all of this. I love the fact that you forgot. You were thinking of yourself, not me for a change." Then he chuckled. "Next time, I'll call first, though. That's an image I only want to see once."

Then he left, still laughing.

I joined Jordan in the kitchen. He had carried in the dishes and was loading them into the dishwasher. I leaned against the counter, watching as he stacked them in an orderly fashion, then reached under the sink and dropped in a pod, studying the controls for a moment before choosing a cycle and shutting the door.

He met my amused glance. "What?"

"Very domesticated."

He chuckled dryly. "I had to learn. To be honest, I enjoyed cooking more than Anna did. I took over the kitchen on the weekends." He held up a finger. "Except for coffee. She made far better coffee."

"I see. Max was hopeless in the kitchen. I remember the time he tried to make garlic bread. I'm certain the fire department has fond memories of it as well."

Jordan threw back his head in amusement. Then he held out his hand. "Can we sit?"

I took his hand and led him back into the living room. We sat on the sofa facing each other.

"Are you okay with Colin?" he asked. "I know his arrival caught us off guard, and it was obvious he had no idea about us."

"Only because I haven't seen him—it wasn't something I wanted to share over the phone. I planned on telling him tonight, except—"

His chuckle interrupted me. "You forgot about tonight."

"I did. This whole week has been so crazy. I guess I've been off-kilter."

He took my hand, holding it within his, making circles on my wrist with his thumb. "Lots to take in."

"Yes."

He released my hand and rubbed his face. I shifted closer, concerned.

"Jordan? What's wrong?"

"I have something to tell you, and it's either going to make you very happy, or you're going to be upset."

"That's a rather large variance."

"I did something."

"Obviously."

He paused and took my hand again. "The house goes up for sale tomorrow. The agent is having an all-day open house on Saturday. She will accept offers as of three o'clock on Tuesday afternoon. She anticipates a bidding war."

"All right."

"I'm fine with selling the house—I really am. But I can't stand the thought of all those people traipsing through the house, making comments."

"Understandable."

"She strongly suggested I not be there." He sucked in some air. "So, I decided to go away for the weekend. I think the break would do me some good."

I tamped down my disappointment that he would be gone. I was looking forward to seeing him at least one day on the weekend, but I understood.

"Are you going to see Gina?"

"No. I decided I wanted to take you to Boston. If you'll come with me."

I blinked. "Boston?"

"They have a great collection of Renoirs on loan again. Some Monets and other impressionists. We could do all the things you never got to do. Spend some time together without boats, grandsons, or BAM boys interrupting us," he added with a wicked grin.

"You want to go to Boston with me? How would we do that?"

"Here's the part where you might get angry with me. I spoke to Bentley. You have tomorrow and Monday off if you want them. You're covered. There's a flight first thing tomorrow and one that gets us home on Monday by lunch. I have the hotel booked, arrangements made for all sorts of fun things for us to do." He squeezed my hand. "And if you don't want, I can cancel it all and I will head to Gina's."

I could only stare. He had arranged all that—on his own?

He shifted closer, his knees pressing against mine. "I don't want to be here this weekend, but I don't want to go to BC, Sandy. I want to take you away. Have days to spend with you—just us. Please come with me."

"You arranged all of this for me?"

He cupped my cheek. "Yes, for you. For us. I wanted to give you something, and I happened to see an advertisement for the Renoir exhibit. I did some checking and then went and spoke to Bentley. He thought it was a great idea and said yes right away."

"Who is going to cover?"

"Emmy was in his office when I got there. She volunteered immediately. Bentley was thrilled. He gets to have Emmy and Addi there with him. Try out the new day care."

"I see." Bentley would love having his girls around him all day.

He looked thoughtful. "I told Bentley it might be time to think of getting you your own assistant. You're so busy all the time."

I had to agree with him. Some days, I could barely keep up. Someone to take away the small stuff would help. But I would discuss that with Bentley at another point.

"And you can go, with everything happening with the house?"

"It's staged and ready. The agent has everything well in hand, and she knows I am gone as of tomorrow. She'll handle the weekend, and if she needs me, I'm as close as the phone. All I have to do is throw a few things in a suitcase."

"You've thought this through very well."

"Are you upset?"

"How can I be upset when you went to so much effort, Jordan?"

"Is that a yes? All you have to do is pack a few things and I'll pick you up in the morning at six. We'll be in Boston before lunchtime, and you'll be staring at Renoirs by two."

"What sort of hotel booking did you make?"

"A suite—two bedrooms," he replied promptly. "No pressure, Sandy."

His gaze was earnest, his words firm. He had no idea how his assurances made me want anything but two bedrooms. His insistence he only wanted time with me solidified the growing feelings I had for him. He was genuine, kind, and unknowingly sexy in his uncertainty. He clasped my hand, fully prepared for me to say no.

Except I didn't want to.

I bent close and brushed a kiss to his cheek. "I would love to go to Boston with you, Jordan."

His happiness was evident. "Really?"

"Yes."

He gripped my shoulders and kissed my mouth. It was a hard, fast pressing of our lips. He did it again, this time holding it longer. Then again with a low groan as he pulled me tight to his chest and kissed me the way he had earlier in the hall. There was barely controlled passion in his caresses and an underlying desire that went straight to my core. I returned his kiss, losing myself in him again.

He eased back. "I need to go home and pack." He dropped another kiss to my mouth. "You have no idea how happy you have made me, my darling."

I thrilled at his endearment. It sounded so right coming from his mouth.

"I'm pretty excited."

"Colin said you would be."

"Colin knows?"

He grinned. "We had quite the fast chat while you were getting dinner. Man-to-man stuff. I told him my idea, and he assured me you would love it." He touched my cheek gently. "Or kill me. He wished me luck either way."

I laughed. That sounded like Colin.

Jordan stood. I gazed up at him. "You won't stay for dessert?"

"Don't you have to pack?"

I glanced at my watch. "It's nine thirty. You can eat dessert and leave by ten. I'll be packed in forty-five minutes. An hour, tops. I think even in my dotage I can handle staying up until eleven."

He pulled me up from the sofa and kissed me again. "Good. I plan on keeping you up late all weekend. Might as well practice now."

I grinned all the way into the kitchen.

I had a feeling I was going to enjoy this surprise weekend.

TWELVE

SANDY

I barely slept all night. Packing was harder than I expected, although I was certain it had more to do with my nerves than the clothes in my closet. I had texted Jordan, asking what sort of clothing I should bring, and his reply hadn't been helpful.

You'll be beautiful in anything. Lots of walking. A nice dress for dinner.

I rolled my eyes at the unclear directive.

How many dinners? One dress-up and the rest casual?

I snorted. He was amazing but also a typical male—short on details.

In the end, I chose some outfits I could mix and match and packed two elegant dresses and one casual one. A good pair of walking shoes and one pair of high heels.

I hesitated over my lingerie drawer. I pulled out a bag that had been stuffed in the corner for months. I let the shimmering ball of satin fall from my fingertips, studying it. Blue, soft, and sexy, it hinted rather than revealed. Perfect for my body at my age. In front of the mirror, I studied myself. I kept in good shape. I wasn't as thin as I once was, but I still had muscle definition, and I looked okay in a bathing suit. My breasts hadn't sagged yet, and my long legs were still lean and shapely. I always tried to play those up. My hair hung past my shoulders, straight, thick, and pure white. I knew Jordan loved to run his fingers through it.

Would he like the nightgown? I had seen it one day while out shopping a couple of months ago, and bought it, then never took it from the bag, wondering in the emptiness of my bedroom why I had purchased it. It had been an impulse buy that seemed silly once I arrived home.

I had no idea if I would need it this weekend. If I was ready to move forward to that step with Jordan. There was no doubt the man had skill when it came to kissing me. He was passionate and confident, his tongue and mouth talented. His long fingers stroked my skin like I was a violin and he a maestro, leaving me longing for more. I lost myself to him, our surroundings fading away, yearning building under my skin and taking over every sense when he had me in his arms.

I tucked the nightgown into the suitcase and added my bathing suit in case.

I was simply being prepared; that was all.

I ignored the fluttering in my stomach at the thought of Jordan seeing me in that nightgown and his reaction.

Then before I could change my mind, I added my toiletry bag and snapped the locks shut. I found my passport and added some American cash to my wallet, grateful I always kept a little on hand.

Now, I was waiting by the door, anxious and already tired. A town car pulled up right at six, and Jordan slipped from the back, meeting me at the door.

He bent down and kissed my cheek. "Hello, my darling."

"Hi."

He picked up my case. "Are you ready?"

I swallowed. "Yes."

He held out his hand. "Let's go."

The airport wasn't overly busy this time of morning, and I wasn't surprised when Jordan directed me to the Executive Class area. We were checked in within minutes and the security line wasn't backed up, so we were in the first-class lounge not long after the car had dropped us off.

We found a table and left our carry-ons. We brought coffee and some pastries back to the table, and Jordan opened his laptop, showing me some of the things we had to choose from.

"We're staying at the Boston Harbor Hotel. I have dinner reservations at Finz tonight and Turner's Seafood tomorrow. Sunday, I thought we could decide if there was anywhere we heard of or simply pick a place."

"Sounds lovely."

"I bought a membership at MFA last night that we'll pick up today. I got tickets for the Impressionists for the three-o'clock time slot." His fingers raced over the keyboard. "We have a cruise on the harbor tomorrow, a walking tour of Salem after dark, but sadly, no baseball game."

"I think I can live without it," I said dryly.

He picked up his coffee. "I thought so."

"Have you booked us every second?" I asked, looking over the itinerary.

He laughed. "No. I saved lots of time for walking, exploring, and shopping."

"You thought of everything."

"I tried. I've never been there before either. I'm excited to share all this with you." A sly grin appeared on his face. "I also booked us a massage Sunday morning."

"Oh god, I love massages."

"Emmy might have told me that." He leaned close, waggled his eyebrows, and spoke in a low, growly voice. "I give *great* massages, Sandy. Play your cards right and maybe I'll show you."

"Is that a fact?"

He brushed his fingers down my cheek. "It is. I'm very *dexterous*." His words were accompanied by another waggle of his eyebrows, his green eyes alive and dancing in the bright light surrounding us.

"Well then," I said, "I suppose I'll have to figure out a way of getting in your good graces."

He linked our fingers together and brought them to his mouth. "You already have, Sandy. You already have."

The flight was uneventful. I napped, my head resting on Jordan's shoulder during the brief trip. The hotel was sumptuous, the suite ready when we arrived. I stood looking out onto the harbor, feeling excited. Our driver had pointed out a lot of landmarks and made some suggestions. I had a feeling it was going to be a fabulous weekend.

Jordan came up behind me, wrapping his arms around my waist and tugging me back to his chest. "Happy?" he murmured.

Without a word, I turned and flung my arms around his neck. I pulled his head down and kissed him. Deeply. Letting him feel my emotions. It had been so long since I had experienced this sort of attention. Being the center of someone's focus. Max's illness prevented him from enjoying life, and although he had been a wonderful husband, I had missed little moments like this for so many years.

Jordan's arms encircled me tightly. His mouth moved with mine, and our tongues danced and teased together. He eased back, smiling down at me. "I love it when *you* kiss *me*," he murmured. "It's a little surprise gift every time."

"I plan on giving you lots of gifts this weekend."

His eyes widened and he ran his finger over my bottom lip. "I look forward it to, my darling. Now, ready to head to the museum?"

"Yes."

"You like this one."

I startled at Jordan's voice. We'd been in the gallery for hours, walking, looking, exploring. I saw paintings I had never seen before. Works of art so beautiful they took my breath away. One

Renoir painting in particular caught my eye, and I kept coming back to it, studying the colors, new hues emerging with every sweep of my gaze. It was called *Landscape on the Coast near Menton*, and I was mesmerized by it.

"Yes."

"What draws you to it?"

"The colors. The light."

Jordan tucked me to his side as people went past. We looked at the painting, not speaking. Then he pressed his lips to my head. "Hmm. The same things I see in you. Beautiful light. Breathtaking colors."

I slapped his arm. "Goof."

He chuckled, capturing my hand. "It's true, Sandy. I see that when I look at you. I see life again."

"Jordan," I breathed out. "I think that is one of the most beautiful things anyone has ever said to me."

"It's the simple truth."

Without thought, I wrapped my hand around his neck and pulled his face down to kiss him. He instantly wrapped his arm around my waist and pulled me in tight. I wasn't a short woman or delicate, but Jordan was tall enough, at times I felt as if I were a piece of Dresden china being carefully cradled within his embrace. It was still an odd feeling, yet I found I liked it.

He released me, smiling. "Should I inquire about purchasing this?" He indicated the painting. "I'm sure I can find forty or fifty million kicking around somewhere."

"Nice little souvenir," I agreed. "But I don't think they sell the paintings off the walls."

"Pity."

I slipped my arm through his. "Let's go see more."

Hours later, my feet were tired from walking, my mind full of all the beauty we'd seen. Outside, the sun was still shining, although the temperature had dropped a little as early evening set in. We waited for the car to arrive, our hands clasped together. "Thank you for today."

Jordan tightened his grip on my fingers. "We can come back if you want. The membership is good for a year, and I can get us tickets to look at the exhibit again this weekend." He lifted my hand to his mouth, kissing my knuckles. "Whatever you want to do this weekend, Sandy. It's yours."

"Dinner," I stated. "I'm starving."

He grinned, opening the car door as it came to a stop in front of us. "Our reservation is in two hours. I have some appetizers waiting at the hotel, and we can get dressed and go."

He thought of everything. "Sounds perfect."

I stepped out from the bedroom, feeling strangely nervous. Jordan turned from the window, and our eyes met across the room. He walked toward me, giving me a chance to take him in. Dressed in a silver-gray suit that clung to his shoulders and suited his coloring, he was handsome. His hair was brushed to gleaming, and his tie matched his green eyes. He stopped in front of me, lifting my hands and kissing them.

"You are beautiful." He grinned widely. "And we match."

I had to laugh. My green dress shot with strands of silver went perfectly with his suit, as if we had coordinated.

Jordan stepped back and twirled his finger. "Let me see."

Feeling like a teenager, I turned in a circle, my full skirt curling around my knees. Jordan shook his head. "You are so sexy, Sandy. Elegant, beautiful, and so, so… *sensual.* It boggles my mind."

My blush threatened. "Thank you."

He crooked his arm. "May I take you to dinner?"

I slipped my arm through his. "Yes."

A few hours later, I sat back with a groan. "I am so full."

Jordan topped up our wine. "It was an amazing meal."

"Amazing," I agreed, then giggled. "So is this wine. I think I might be a little drunk."

"I think we both are."

The evening had been wonderful. The ambiance of the restaurant, Jordan's company, our conversation—everything.

"You are the perfect date."

He lifted his eyebrows. "Perfect?"

I leaned forward, stroking my finger along his hand. He had strong hands. Large, capable of performing the most manual of tasks or touching me with the gentlest of caresses. "I can talk to you about anything. You never judge me."

He cocked his head to the side. "I'm interested in anything you want to tell me, Sandy. I feel the same way about you. I enjoy our conversations."

"You make me feel safe."

He flipped his hand up and encased mine. "You are safe with me."

"It's been a long time since I felt that way."

"I imagine so. I know the feeling of caring for an ill spouse. Nothing feels safe anymore. Nothing feels right. Your entire world is upside down, especially when you know they will be taken from you at some point and there's nothing you can do." He was quiet. "You offer me that safety as well, Sandy. I feel very peaceful with you."

"Why did you put my bag in the master bedroom and yours in the other one?" I blurted out.

His smile was gentle. "I thought you'd like to soak in that huge tub. It didn't matter to me what room I had, as long as you were happy. This weekend is all about you, my darling."

His words, his thoughtfulness, his very closeness soaked into my soul.

I met his gaze directly. "What if what would make me happy was both of us in that room?"

There was a moment of silence. The pulse in his neck beat rapidly as he studied me. "Is that the wine talking?"

"No. It's my heart."

His grip on my hand tightened, and his eyes darkened. "Then I would signal for the check, and hurry back to the hotel to have you alone. In my arms."

"Then pay the bill, Jordan."

He signaled for the waiter.

We held hands in the car, Jordan's thumb drawing restless circles on my skin. We didn't attempt to make small talk or sit too close. Both of us were wavering on the sharp edge of desire, each caught up in our own thoughts and working through the varied emotions this moment was drawing out.

In the hotel room, we circled each other, unsure and on edge. Jordan held out his hand, then tugged me into his arms. "Let me sleep beside you tonight, Sandy. Just hold you. We don't have to rush it."

I nodded against his chest, unable to speak. I wanted more than to sleep beside him, but I didn't know how to form the words.

He kissed the top of my head. "Go get ready, and I'll join you."

I changed into the pretty nightgown I had bought. Washed my face and brushed my teeth. I released my hair from its chignon and let it fall past my shoulders. I studied my image in the mirror. I was pale, my eyes bright in my face.

I stepped into the bedroom. Jordan swung around, whatever he was about to say dying on his lips. He stared at me, his eyes dark, his body tense. He was in a robe, his chest and legs bare. I felt myself flush, the heat building under my skin as I wondered if he was totally naked underneath.

"I turned down the bed," he murmured.

I stepped forward, confused when he stepped back. He shook his head. "I don't know if this is such a good idea."

"Why?"

"Because you look so sexy and inviting in that pretty little night-gown. So sexy, in fact, I want to see it in a ball on the floor. I want to touch you, Sandy. Everywhere. Kiss you." I watched, fascinated, as his hands curled into fists at his sides as if he was holding them in place. "I don't think I can sleep beside you when what I really want to do is make love to you. I want to make you mine."

His words were clipped, his voice low and gruff. His robe hung in long folds of terry cloth, but I saw the evidence of his desire. Heard the want and need in his voice. Felt the proof of his struggle in his tense stance.

I knew he was right. I didn't want to sleep beside him either—at least not yet. Without thought, I lifted my arms and tugged the nightgown I was wearing over my head. I tossed it, watching as it landed in a shimmering pool of blue at his feet.

"Then come and take what you want, Jordan."

JORDAN

I was transfixed by the beauty in front of me. Sandy clothed was elegant, refined, and unknowingly sexy. It was in the tilt of her head, the sway of her hips as she walked, the undone buttons at her throat that hinted at the hidden skin.

Naked, she was a vision of wanton sex. Proud, her shoulders back, her full breasts round with dark pink aureole and hard-tipped nipples, she stood in front of me like a gift from heaven. My erection that had been growing steadily kicked up, a pulsating need overtaking me I hadn't felt for a long time.

Sandy watched me with hooded eyes. I knew how much nerve it had taken for her to make the first move. She awed me with her act of courage. Neither of us was seventeen with the blush of youth and the unblemished bodies of a teenager anymore. We both carried our life on our skin, within our hearts, and in the memories of the past.

Sandy's body was lovely. Her skin glowed, taut and soft. There was a softness to her hips, a slight roundness to her stomach. Her breasts were high and sexy, the indent at her waist clear and defined.

And her legs. Her long, lovely legs I suddenly needed wrapped around me as we moved together. She had them crossed demurely in front of her, hiding her most personal of secrets, making me wait to discover all of her.

But I planned on that wait being a short one.

Our gazes held as I walked toward her. I ran my finger along her collarbone, back and forth, smiling as color flushed her skin and her breathing picked up. I trailed my hand down her arm, softly teasing the juncture of her elbow, ghosting it down her forearm, tracing it in circles on her palm, then back up. I heard her soft whimper as I circled her. Saw the shiver run through her body. I opened my robe and pressed myself against her as I drew her into the warmth of the material and my torso. She let her head fall against my chest and I pushed her heavy hair away, nuzzling her neck.

"You are beyond beautiful, my darling. I want you so badly, Sandy."

She turned in my arms, making me groan. Our bodies meshed together, her suppleness melding against mine. Her breasts rubbed the coarse hairs on my chest, her hard nipples teasing my skin. She lifted her arms, wrapping them around my neck.

"My turn," she whispered, pushing my robe from my shoulders. I helped her, shrugging off the white robe and letting it hit the floor. She drew a single finger over my chest, down my arm, mimicking my earlier actions. When she cupped my erection through my boxers, I dropped my head back with a long moan.

"Take me to bed, Jordan."

I didn't need to be asked twice. I lifted her into my arms, making her gasp then giggle as I carried her to the bed, placing her on the mattress. I followed her, my body pressing her down into the thick covering as I captured her mouth. We kissed endlessly. Long and hard. Soft and gentle. Exploring and discovering each other. Tasting and learning.

I couldn't stop touching her everywhere with my hands and my mouth. I discovered the slope of her shoulder, the elegant length of her throat, the spot behind her ear that made her shiver. Her nipples were firm peaks as I tongued and sucked them, making her groan. Her hips fit perfectly in my hands.

She was ticklish behind her knees, her shapely calves strong and smooth under my touch. I ghosted my fingers up her thighs, laughing as she sat up, pushing me back and demanding her turn to explore.

It had been a long time since anyone had explored my body—and I enjoyed every second of it. Her tongue was talented and inquisitive as she traced it over my ribs, up my neck, and along my jaw. She used her sharp teeth to nip at my ears, tease the juncture where neck met shoulder, and nibbled at my chest. She tongued my nipples then slipped lower to my stomach.

"You are so defined," she murmured against my skin. "So sexy, Jordan."

"Aiden and Van keep me in shape."

She sat back on my thighs, her eyes locked on mine as she traced over my aching erection. "Is this for me?"

I groaned as she slipped her hand inside my boxers and wrapped her fingers around me. "Yes," I choked out.

She stroked me, her eyes glittering in the muted lighting of the room. "So hard, Jordan. So...*big*." Her finger circled the crown. "I can't wait to feel you inside me."

Her words released something inside me. With a low growl, I had her under me, our mouths fused together. She yanked at my boxers, then used her feet to drag them down my legs, pushing them off impatiently. She opened her legs, and I settled into the cradle of her body, feeling the heat of her surround me. The blunt head of my cock rubbed against her, the slickness of her making me groan.

I pushed up on my elbows, meeting her eyes. "It's been six years for me, Sandy."

"It's been almost four for me." She sighed. "And it was very sparse before that. With Max's age and his medical condition, our physical relationship was limited to cuddles a lot of the time."

I nodded. It had been the same in the last stage of Anna's illness. I knew Sandy had lived with Max's deteriorating health and the large age gap for longer. We both understood what the other had experienced. I kissed her gently. "I know," I assured her.

Her lips curled into a sexy smirk. "Is this our safety talk? I'm too old to get pregnant."

I pushed back a strand of hair from her flushed cheek. She was gorgeous with her mussed hair spread on the pillow, her lips swollen from mine, and her skin warm and glowing. I had to smile at her teasing words. "I had a vasectomy years ago," I told her. "I do have condoms if you feel better."

She wrapped her legs around me, bringing me farther into her warmth. "No. Just you."

With a groan, I lifted her hips and thrust forward. She opened for me like petals opening for the morning sun. I was surrounded, the heat of her scorching me in the best way possible. Inch by inch, I sank into her until we were flush. I stilled, the moment and its significance overwhelming.

I opened my eyes and met her hazel gaze. Her eyes were brimming with emotion. "You're mine now, my darling."

"Show me," she whispered.

I began to move. Long, languid strokes, our bodies joining together in a rhythm as old as time. There was no screaming or thrashing. There was passion, a deep abiding connection we both felt. We kissed endlessly, murmuring words of adoration, promises whispered against slick skin as we rocked together, the pleasure so intense, I felt as if I would burn alive with it.

Sandy's sounds were erotic. Low whimpers, pleading moans, my name sighed out in long breathless gasps. I moved and thrust, kissed every inch of her skin I could, clutched her to me as my body began to shake. She grasped my shoulders, drew her legs higher, moved with me as if we'd done this a hundred times before. She anchored me to her as I reached my pinnacle, shouting out her name, thrusting deeper, gripping her hips as I shook and begged.

"Come with me, Sandy. Please...please," I pleaded.

She cried out, her hold tightening on my neck, her voice imploring and shaking. Long forgotten tendrils of ecstasy swirled around me, sending me to a place somewhere outside my body. We were slick with sweat, the room filled with our cries, nothing outside this moment mattering anymore. It was me claiming Sandy, and her cementing herself into my heart. My body now belonged to her, as well as my soul.

From now on, everything I had was hers.

I collapsed onto her body, my breathing loud and ragged. Sandy's chest rose and fell rapidly, her arms holding me tightly. Carefully, I rolled, taking her with me, holding her close.

The room was quiet aside from our breathing. "Are you all right, my darling?"

She nuzzled my neck. "I'm good."

"That was—" I swallowed, trying to find the right way to say it "—I have no words for how amazing that was."

She laughed low in her throat. She tilted up her head, meeting my gaze. She looked beautiful—tired, sated, and well loved—but beautiful.

"It was," she agreed, tracing a finger over my lips. "We were amazing."

I kissed the tip of her finger. "This changes everything."

She smiled. "You never mince words, do you, love?"

Her endearment touched something deep in my heart. I kissed her lovingly, nuzzling her lips. "Not when it comes to you, no. You mean too much to me."

She snuggled closer. "I'm good with that."

It was still too soon for declarations of love. Our actions showed it, and we both felt it, but the words would be spoken another time.

For now, she was in my arms, and I had no plans on letting her go.

I was good with that.

THIRTEEN

JORDAN

Waking up with Sandy beside me felt as if I were waking to a different world. The last four years, the start of each day contained a small piece of heartbreak when my eyes would open and I realized all over again I was alone.

This morning Sandy was with me. I could smell her light fragrance. Feel the softness of her hair tickle my chin.

There was no heartache, only a sense of rightness. And when I opened my eyes and met her sleepy hazel gaze, I smiled. Her answering smile warmed me. The feel of her body so closely entwined with mine woke other parts of me.

She lifted her head, reaching for me, and we came together. Affectionate kisses, murmured words of assurance, and long, slow movements as we joined, seeking each other's mouths, tasting and exploring. The feel of us was still new and exciting. Heady and rich. The moments of discovery new and wonderful. Being cradled inside her, surrounded by her heat, was thrilling. Hearing her whisper my name in a long, breathless moan as I moved within her was a turn-on. She was passionate and giving. She liked to be talked to while we made love, her response to my voice pushing us both closer to the edge.

"You are so lovely," I murmured. "So sexy."

"Yes, Sandy, touch me like that. Just like that," I encouraged.

"Say my name, my darling. Say it."

"Come for me, please. I want to feel you," I begged.

She lay in my arms in the aftermath, her heat soaking into my body, both of us at peace. I ran my fingertips up and down her arm, pressed endless kisses to her head. She stroked my chest, resting her hand against my neck as she sighed in contentment. It was intimate and right.

We were right.

Over breakfast, we mapped out our day. Sandy talked about all the places she wanted to go, and I scanned the various sites, scheduling around the boat cruise and our evening tour of Salem. Once our day was planned, I sat back and studied her. Sitting at the table, wrapped in a fluffy robe, with her hair gathered up in a knot, askew and messy, Sandy glowed. She was nibbling on a croissant, one leg tucked under her, without a trace of makeup on.

"You are incredibly beautiful."

She looked up, that flush of color I loved pooling on her cheeks. "Stop it," she murmured, picking up her coffee.

"You really are. I've always thought so, but this morning, you're simply exquisite."

She tilted her head, looking impish.

"This morning? I'm a mess. My hair isn't done, I have no makeup on, and I'm not even dressed."

I picked up her hand and kissed it. "And yet, you have never looked more beautiful to me."

Her cheeks darkened further.

"You're not so bad yourself, Jordan. You hide quite the body under your business clothes." She sipped her coffee. "Very sexy."

"I'm glad it pleases you. I enjoy my workouts with Van and Aiden. Keeps me young."

She picked up her croissant. "And strong." She winked, looking mischievous. "Your, ah, *stamina* is impressive."

"Well, as the song goes, I'm not as good as I once was, but I'm as good once as I ever was."

She lifted a shoulder, a smile curling her lips. "I'll take quality over quantity, Jordan. Grade A filet is far better than a run-of-the-mill hamburger."

I threw back my head in laughter. "You have a way with words this morning, my darling."

I loved seeing her this way. Relaxed, happy, at ease with me. Tousled and sexy across the breakfast table. It was something I wanted to see every day.

I leaned across the table and kissed her. "Ready to go have another amazing day?"

She smiled against my mouth. "Yes."

"Okay."

The day passed in a long string of smiles. The harbor cruise was a hit with both of us. We stood out on the deck, enjoying the sun and breeze. The boat wasn't crowded, and we enjoyed the tour and the vistas. Sandy stood in front of me, and I wrapped my arms around her. She took some pictures. We saw forts, shipwrecks, lighthouses—all of which delighted her. She glanced up at me.

"This is so amazing!"

Unable to resist, I kissed her. She caught my head in her hand, curling her fingers into my hair as our mouths moved together. When I pulled away, her cheeks were flushed, and she touched her lips. I wonder if she knew she did that after we kissed.

As I had discovered, much to my delight, Sandy liked to be kissed. She also loved being held and staying close when we strolled. Our hands were entwined most of the time, and if she would drift away to look at an item, as soon as she returned, she held her hand out for mine. She was such a strong force at the office, having her share this private, personal side of herself with me was humbling. It proved to me she trusted me.

She rested against me, laying her hand over my arms. "Thank you, Jordan, for bringing me here."

I kissed her head. No words were necessary.

We strolled around in Boston Common. Toured Samuel Adams brewery and tasted many samples, discovered a small market, and did some shopping. We had dinner at Turner's, enjoying the bustling atmosphere of the restaurant.

"Oh my god," Sandy moaned. "You have to taste this."

I opened my mouth and let her slide in a piece of swordfish, chewing it slowly.

"That is delicious."

I slid my plate in her direction. "You have to try the lobster pie."

She speared a forkful and lifted it to her mouth. She closed her eyes in appreciation. "Wow."

I nodded. "I know. Good thing we're walking so much. Otherwise, I'd gain twenty pounds this weekend. Between the chowders, the crab cakes, beer, and the snacks we keep having..." I trailed off.

Sandy winked, trying her best to look lewd. "I'm sure later we can think of another way to burn off some more *calories*," she whispered in a breathless voice, then quirked her eyebrows.

I began to laugh. All day, she had delighted me with her sense of humor. I knew she was intelligent and well-read. I expected to enjoy her company, but her surprisingly ribald jokes, her amusing imitations of a Boston accent, and cheeky remarks had me in stitches several times. I couldn't recall laughing this much for a long time.

"I might take you up on that."

"I guess I had better get dessert then, just to keep up my strength."

"Good idea."

I glanced at my phone. "The latest weather update says it's supposed to rain all day tomorrow. Maybe you'd like to go back to the MFA."

"I'd love that." She ate in silence for a few moments, then spoke. "Um, how bad is the rain supposed to be?"

I rechecked my phone. "Storms overnight and then rain most of the day."

"Oh."

Something in her tone made me tense. That one word indicated anxiety. I reached across the table and took her hand.

"What is it, my darling?"

She shrugged, looking self-conscious. "It's silly."

"I doubt that. Now, tell me."

"I hate storms. They frighten me."

"A lot of people share that fear. It's not silly."

"I hate the turbulence they cause. The noise and the wind. All of it."

"Well then, I guess I'll have to hold you extra tight. You can use me as a shield. And we don't have to leave the hotel tomorrow at all."

"Just rain doesn't bother me. In fact, I find the sound of rain quite soothing."

"All right, we'll play it by ear and see what the weather does."

She met my eyes, gratitude swimming in her gaze. "Thank you."

"All you have to do is tell me, Sandy. Whatever you need, however you're feeling, I'm here."

She squeezed my hand. "I'm so glad you are."

"Good."

At the hotel, I could feel her tension. I had a massage booked for us in the morning, but I had the feeling another one wouldn't be objected to at the moment. I gathered some lotion and towels in the bathroom and instructed her to don one of the fluffy white robes the hotel provided and asked her to put up her hair. I sat in the large armchair and tossed a cushion on the floor.

"Sit." I pointed to the pillow.

She did as I asked, then laughed quietly as I bent over her, tugging on the sash of the robe. "I need access," I teased, dropping a kiss to her neck.

She loosened the robe, and I pushed it off her shoulders, running my hands along her soft skin, feeling the tension under the skin.

"Wow."

She sighed, letting her head hang down. "My shoulders have been described as cement."

"Well, let's see what I can do about that."

I added some lotion to my hands and began to knead her tight muscles. She groaned low in her throat, but it wasn't a groan of pain. I worked at the stiffness, massaging and stroking, feeling her beginning to relax. I talked about silly things. The couple we'd seen taking selfies along the pier. A sculpture we'd both guessed at, trying to determine exactly what it represented and being wrong. Amusing little stories about Van, the boys, funny things my kids did as they grew up. Anything to distract her as the storm outside drew closer. I wanted her to concentrate on my voice, the feel of my hands. Slowly, her muscles loosened, her shoulders sagging. I tipped up her head, stroking her neck and along the front of her chest, over her collarbone, keeping my touch light and gentle. She kept her eyes shut, a small smile on her face.

I tried not to notice her breasts but failed. Badly. The fullness of them I could see perfectly from my vantage point. How slowly her nipples were tightening. How my groin tightened in response. With a casual sigh, she lifted her arms, draping them over my widened knees, pushing her breasts out. I drifted my hands lower, touching her. Stroking over her nipples with my thumbs as I cupped her. She whimpered, a soft small sound, opening her eyes. I met her gaze and smiled as she wrapped one arm around my neck, drawing me down to her mouth. I kissed her, upside down, leisurely, our tongues meeting and withdrawing, my hands still on her breasts.

"Jordan," she whispered.

"Tell me what you want, my darling. Tell me, and it's yours."

"You. I want you."

"Here or in the bedroom?"

In one fluid movement, she was on her feet, her robe a discarded cloud of white at her feet.

"Right here, in this chair."

My erection kicked up, straining against my zipper. Sandy watched me with hooded eyes as I smiled, leaned back, and opened my hands in invitation.

"Take me however you want me."

She never broke eye contact as she tugged on my zipper and yanked off my pants. I helped her with my shirt, impatient to feel her skin against mine.

Then she settled on my lap, straddling me. Our mouths fused

115

together, and I held her close, feeling the delicate beauty of her back under my fingers.

She shifted, lifting and settling herself, my cock at her entrance. We both moaned as she lowered herself, taking me inside slowly. Flush together, she gripped my shoulders, taking her hair out of her clip, shaking it loose around her shoulders. She shuddered as I thrust into her.

"You feel so good, Jordan. So good."

"So do you." I groaned as she rolled her hips. "So do you."

"We're both going to feel even better," she whispered, then began to move. She gripped the back of my neck, clutching the arm of the chair with her other hand. She undulated over me, her movements smooth and graceful. She arched her back as I nuzzled her breasts, moaned as I pulled her closer, burying my face in her neck as she rode me. I praised her, begged her, uttered a curse or two as she took control and brought me more pleasure than I thought possible. I gripped her hips as she began to cry out, thrusting into her, shouting her name, and coming hard.

She collapsed against my chest, shuddering in the afterglow, her arms wrapped around my neck and her body fluid and warm next to mine.

I kissed her head. "Wow, my darling. That was simply..." I trailed off, unable to find words to adequately describe what had just occurred between us.

"That was fucking awesome," she murmured.

I burst out laughing. Sandy rarely swore, and I found it rather endearing when she did. And if I was being honest, a bit of a turn-on —especially given the reason for her cursing.

I stood, taking her with me. She clung to me, smiling as I set her on her feet in the shower. "Let's clean up and go to bed." I kissed her lips. "We can cuddle."

"I like cuddling with you."

"Good. Me too."

She did hate storms. It finally started around two, the thunder beginning to rumble and lightning flashing. The rain was heavy, hitting the glass outside like small pebbles.

Sandy had fallen asleep for a while, worn out from the day and no doubt, our rather vigorous lovemaking, but she woke at the first far-off rumble of thunder, her body tense. She nestled closer, seeking the shelter of my embrace, and I held her tight, trying to offer what security I could.

She trembled in my arms, her face buried in my chest, small sounds of distress escaping her mouth every so often. I talked to her, smoothing my hands up and down her back in calming passes, whispering words of comfort. I had never seen her so vulnerable. Unsure how else to console her, I began to hum. I always loved to sing to my kids, and I tended to hum under my breath without realizing it. Van teased me about it all the time. When Anna was ill and unable to sleep, I would hum to her—she said she found it soothing and it helped her to rest.

After a while, Sandy relaxed, snuggling closer, but without the tension I had felt in her before. I felt her body grow heavier with sleep and I kept going. I hummed and stroked her hair, enjoying the fact that she was relying on me and that I was helping her.

The storm continued, but she slept, safe and peaceful in my embrace. I hummed until the storm abated, the sounds fading off, leaving only the rain.

Knowing she was resting, I drifted off to sleep, keeping my arms around her. I wondered how to get her to agree to sleep beside me every night. I had a feeling I was going to miss the feel of her next to me once this weekend was over.

SANDY

I paused in front of my favorite Renoir painting again, standing across from it and staring. Something about the colors and light drew me in. Jordan was wandering in another section, but he would know where to find me.

I smiled as I thought about him.

Jordan.

This weekend had been more incredible than I could have imagined. We traveled well together, at ease with each other, and both enjoying the same things. I loved walking with him, often stopping to look at something that caught my eye or popping into a store. He was endlessly patient, never rushing me. He stayed close on our explorations, holding my hand, tucking me into his side. On our Salem walking tour, he had guided me around dips in the sidewalk, low spots in the grass as we followed the group.

The approaching storm made me jumpy, but he kept an eye on the weather and had us back at the hotel long before the storm began.

His massage and the ardent lovemaking that ensued had been one of the most pleasurable experiences of my life. He had no problem with me taking control, his green eyes dark with desire, his warm voice encouraging me as I rode him. I loved watching him lose control. The way his head fell back, his neck muscles tightened as he groaned and murmured in pleasure. How he praised and cajoled as we made love. The way he called my name. His deep, fervent, soul-drugging kisses that thrilled me to the core.

His understanding about my fear of storms was typical Jordan. He accepted it, didn't make me feel silly for being frightened, and when the storm descended on us, held me close as he promised and kept me safe. When he began to hum, my entire body relaxed. He had a deep, rich tone that soothed me, and combined with his close proximity, he accomplished something which had never happened before. I fell asleep and stayed asleep as the storm raged. Without a nightmare. When I woke up, it was dawn, Jordan was still beside me, his arms a protective shield, and I was fine.

When he woke, we made love again. Sleepy and warm, our movements were unhurried, our kisses long and gentle. He was an amazing lover—giving and patient, talented with his tongue and fingers. I had forgotten the joys of lovemaking. The passionate movements, the sensation of a strong body joined with mine, the pleasure building between us. The whispers and groans. The feel of fingers and lips skimming along my skin. The way the air around us heated, the world shrinking down to the two bodies joined in a dance as old as time.

The massage he had booked this morning was wonderful, but the capable hands of the masseuse had nothing on Jordan's touch.

Jordan was skilled and passionate. He surprised me with taut muscles and incredible stamina, the way his eyes darkened as he explored my body. The low curses that fell from his lips in the height of passion, the sounds erotic and sexy. He was simply incredible.

Movement caught my eye, and I shifted my gaze to see Jordan headed my way. Tall, handsome, and confident, he strode toward me, a smile meant only for me on his face.

I returned his smile with my own.

Simply incredible, and even more incredible, he was mine.

He reached my side, sliding an arm around my waist and dropping a kiss to my head. "I knew I'd find you here."

"Having one last look at *Landscape on the Coast near Menton.*"

He laughed low in his throat. "It's part of the permanent collection," he assured me. "We'll visit again."

I hugged his arm. "Thank you."

He patted my hand affectionately. "Anytime."

Despite the rain, we strolled the streets, dry under a large umbrella Jordan purchased. We found a lovely little bistro and had an early dinner, then headed back to the hotel. We enjoyed each other's quiet company while I read on my Kindle and Jordan worked on a crossword puzzle. He did them in pen, thoughtfully tapping the nib on his chin as he pondered a word. I liked watching him—the way he furrowed his brow, mouthed a word, or shook his head when he figured out a particularly difficult clue. I had asked him if he ever made a mistake. He had glanced up at me over the rim of his reading glasses, looking sensual and amused.

"No," was his simple answer.

Eventually, I ended up in the massive tub, surrounded by foam and warm water. I floated, mindless and serene. Jordan strolled in, placing a glass of wine on the ledge. He turned to leave, but I grabbed his hand.

"You could join me." I winked. "I could wash your back."

"Is that a fact?"

I nodded, lifting the loofah sponge high. My breast peeked out from the foam, and I grinned. "Oops."

He lifted one eyebrow, a smirk tugging at his lips. "Sandy, are you seducing me?"

I fluttered my eyelashes. "Is it working?"

He yanked his shirt over his head. "Damn right."

Seconds later, he was in the tub with me, dragging me close in the warm water. He wrapped his legs around me, lifting mine over his hips and bringing me flush to him. His erection was already hard and pressed between us, and I whimpered at the feel of him. He yanked me to his chest, running his lips up my neck to my ear. "See what you do to me, my darling?" He nipped at my neck. "One glimpse of your sexy body all wet and naked, and I'm hard." He cursed low in his throat as I rolled my hips. *"Fuck,* Sandy, I want you."

Hearing him curse, lose control of his gentlemanly, polite ways, did something to me. He grasped my neck, drawing my face to his and kissed me. Endless moments passed as we lost ourselves to the growing passion. I ached with my need for him, longing to feel him inside me. I gripped the edges of the tub, lifting myself up, then lowering down on his hardness, inch by inch. I never broke eye contact, letting him see the pleasure I felt. When we were flush, when he was buried so deep inside me it was as if we were one, I leaned close to his ear. "Take me, Jordan."

He grabbed my hips, setting the pace. This wasn't the gentle lovemaking I'd experienced with him all weekend. It wasn't me who had control this time either. This was fast, hard, and intense. He licked at my neck, sucked my breasts, and drove into me like a man possessed. I felt claimed. Sexy. Powerful.

The water rose and fell with us, long waves of desire as Jordan grunted and moved. It splashed over the edge of the tub, hitting the floor in loud droplets. Jordan's grip tightened, and he tugged me close, his face falling in my neck. "Now, Sandy. Please come with me."

I was so close, my body strung tight with desire. Jordan slipped his hand between us, touching me where I needed it, and I cried out, locking down as he joined me, his guttural moan echoing in the room. His movements quickened, and then he shouted my name.

We stilled, my head falling to his shoulder as he gathered me close, pressing a kiss to my forehead. After a few moments, I unlocked my legs and slid back. We regarded each other with lazy smiles on our faces, both too exhausted and too sated to talk much.

Finally, I peeked over the edge of the tub.

"Good thing we have lots of towels."

Jordan handed me the glass of wine, his expression one of fond amusement. "Good thing we didn't knock this over."

I sipped the cool liquid, enjoying the bite of the pinot.

Jordan rubbed my legs. "You all right?"

I winked at him. "Not sure I'll be able to walk tomorrow, but I'm fine."

"I was a little rough. I got carried away," he admitted.

"I liked it." I enjoyed being able to take control when I wanted or to release it to him. Either way, our lovemaking was spectacular. Together, we somehow meshed, sharing a passion that flamed hot and bright when we were alone.

He sighed and moved back, leaning on the other end of the tub. Our legs pressed together, his toes idly stroking my skin. He rested his arms on the edge of the tub, the water clinging to his skin.

"At my age, that doesn't happen very often."

I lifted one shoulder. "Then I'm glad I was here when it did."

He bent at the waist, his expression serious. "It will only be you when it happens next time, Sandy." He relaxed back, picking up my foot and massaging the instep. I groaned as his fingers worked, easing the tightness of the arch. He was right when he told me he gave great massages. I could get used to it very easily.

"And the time after," he added with a wink.

I smiled, wiggling my toes. "You're saying, fast or slow, I'm stuck with you?"

He squeezed my foot. "Yes."

"Okay. Good to know."

FOURTEEN

SANDY

It started on the plane ride home. That niggling little voice I couldn't quite hear, whispering in my head. I had the feeling I had forgotten something—something important. Mentally, I went through the hotel suite. I had my clothes, my Kindle, and was certain I had remembered to pack all the souvenirs and mementos we had purchased, including a gorgeous shawl Jordan had insisted on buying for me at the gift shop at MFA. It was the softest cashmere, in the most vivid shades of blue and green I had ever seen. Light and warm, it was still in its wrappings, but it was the first thing I had put into my case.

I racked my brain, then decided if it was that important, I would have Jordan contact the hotel to send on to me. Otherwise, I would replace it.

Still, that nagging feeling wouldn't leave. Jordan slept on the short flight, but I was unable to settle. I checked my messages and email, somehow not shocked that my work profile showed nothing pending. Emmy was efficient and no doubt kept up with everything Bentley needed. Knowing him, he put aside some things for me to deal with so she wouldn't be overloaded. I had a feeling the two of them would have spent a great deal of time together in the day care. They were enraptured with their daughter, and Bentley was especially besotted. It was lovely to see how much he had changed. Emmy was good for him.

It was wonderful to know all my boys were settling down, finding the right person to share their lives with. I wondered how many BAM babies would appear over the next few years—I was looking forward to being part of their futures.

Max and I never had children. He'd had a vasectomy before he met me, and although he attempted to have it reversed, it didn't work. We were refused adoption because of Max's age, and the one attempt we made to adopt privately ended in disaster and disappointment, and I swore I wouldn't go through that again.

Meeting Bentley and the boys had given me the ability to love and care for someone other than Max. They eased the heartache of never being a mother—especially when Reid came along. His history and pain provoked a deep maternal response in me, and I adored him.

They all treated me as their adoptive mother since none of them had a motherly influence in their lives. And our grandson, Colin, held a very special place in my heart. I had held him as a baby, watched him grow, and loved him as fiercely as a mother would.

All my boys made the small part of my heart that ached for a child a little less painful. They filled a void not even Max could touch.

I shook my head at my thoughts. I rubbed my temples as the odd sensation of something forgotten, something lost, ran down my spine.

"Are you all right, my darling?" Jordan's voice broke through my odd musings.

I startled at his voice but forced a smile to my face. "Yes, of course."

"You've gone pale. Are you feeling ill?"

"No. You checked the hotel suite before we left, didn't you?"

"Yes. Why? Do you think you forgot something?"

"I have an odd feeling I did."

"I can ask the hotel to check if it's important."

I waved it off. "It's probably my toothbrush. I think I can get by."

He lifted my hand to kiss it, but for some odd reason, I resisted. He frowned but patted my hand instead, leaving his warm palm to rest on top of my hand. "We'll figure it out."

I nodded in silence and turned to the window, fighting the impulse not to pull my hand away.

What on earth was going on with me?

With a sigh, I shut my eyes. I must be tired from the weekend.
That had to be it.

J ordan carried my bag up the steps, waiting as I unlocked the
porch door, then the inner door. He followed me in, setting
down my bag.

I dropped my keys in the bowl, suddenly tense and unsure. I had
no idea what to say to him.

He studied me for a moment. "Are you sure you're all right?"

"I'm fine."

"You seem...distracted. Or upset."

I sighed. "A bit tired." I lifted one shoulder, unsure how to explain
the unease I was feeling. "Maybe a little sad the weekend is done. Back
to reality now," I added lightly.

He stepped closer, sliding an arm around my waist. Before I could
protest, he drew me close, enveloping me in his warmth. The clean
scent of him filled my nose, and with a long breath, I relaxed into him,
wondering why I had resisted his comfort earlier.

"I think reality is a little different for each of us now," he
murmured. "At least, I hope you know that." He pressed a kiss to my
head. "Get some rest and I'll call you later."

I nodded. He eased back, looking down at me. He bent and
brushed a kiss to my cheek. "Call me if you need anything, all right?"

"I will."

He paused before he walked out the door.

"I'm not sure how I'll sleep without you beside me tonight, Sandy."
He shook his head. "I'm not looking forward to it."

He walked out, pulling the door tight behind him.

I stared after his retreating figure, the unease back. My stomach
tightened, and my body became tense.

That odd sensation crept over me, causing a shiver to run down
my spine.

Somehow, without Jordan beside me, I felt nervous, worried, and unsure.

I picked up my bag, mentally giving myself a good shake.

"Stop it, Sandy. You're just tired."

That mantra repeated itself in my head for the next few hours.

I was restless the remainder of the day. I unpacked, checking everything, reassuring myself I hadn't forgotten anything of importance, yet the feeling lingered. For some reason, I carried all the things we had bought, including the lovely shawl, into the room I used as an office. It had always been my space, decorated with a feminine touch. Max rarely came in except to ask a question or, in our earlier years, to bring me a glass of wine or a cup of coffee. It had simply been a place I could go to on my own. I wasn't sure why I brought the bags in here, but I felt better once I had.

I did a few chores, made some toast I nibbled on, then paced the house in an endless loop. I couldn't settle, no matter how I tried. My book held no interest for me, there was nothing on TV, and the music I had playing bothered more than soothed, so I shut it off.

Jordan called in the early evening, his voice a welcome distraction.

"How are you?"

"Fine," I assured him. "Just having a quiet evening."

There was a pause, and I wondered if he was waiting for me to tell him I missed him. I wanted to, but somehow, the words stuck in my throat.

"Any news from the real estate agent?" I asked.

He cleared his throat. "Yes, she dropped by after I got home. The open house was a huge success, and she expects a lot of offers tomorrow."

"That is good news."

"Well, it will be interesting, that's for sure."

"I'm sure it will be fine."

"Gina called as well. She wants to come in a few weeks to go through the boxes at the warehouse. She's trying to coordinate her trip with Warren's, so they come at the same time." He paused. "I think they want to spare me going through things twice."

"That is thoughtful."

"Yes. I was thinking, perhaps we could all have dinner one night."

His words hung in the air. He wanted to introduce me to his children—officially. I had met them at the office on different occasions, but under vastly diverse circumstances. As a married coworker, not the woman he was having an affair with.

Internally, I shook my head. I was more than that to Jordan. I knew that without a doubt—why had those words gone through my head? We weren't having an affair. We were in a relationship.

"Sandy?" Jordan's worried voice prompted me.

"Sorry," I laughed, trying not to convey my sudden discomfort. "I was daydreaming."

"So, dinner?"

"Yes, we'll have to arrange that."

"Sandy, my darling, what's wrong?"

"Nothing is wrong."

"Then why am I sensing a huge distance from you?"

"I'm simply tired, Jordan. We had a busy weekend, and I'm exhausted."

"It was a wonderful weekend, I thought."

"Yes," I agreed, although my tone was odd. "Wonderful."

"Sandy—"

I cut him off, not liking the solicitous tone in his voice or the edge of hurt it contained. I hated knowing it was me who put that hurt there.

"Jordan, I have to go. My tub will be overflowing. I'll see you at the office."

Before he could reply, I hung up.

I stared at the phone, fighting with myself. I wanted to pick it up and call him back. Tell him about the odd feeling I couldn't shake. Ask him to come get me. He would sit with me and talk it through—help me make sense of the unease and worry I was feeling.

Twice, I picked up the phone, then set it back in the charger.

How could I explain it to Jordan, when I didn't understand it myself?

I ran a hand over my hair and stood. Maybe a bath was a good idea. Then I would head to bed and get a good night's sleep. Things would look better in the morning.

I tossed and turned, my sleep fractured and filled with dark, twisted dreams. My bedroom felt oppressive and hot. I flung off the covers and switched on the light, glancing at the clock. It was just after three. I should be asleep, but I felt twitchy and anxious.

I got up and pulled on my robe. I went to the kitchen and poured a glass of ice water, needing to feel the cold. I sipped it, wandering around the house, switching on lights as I did. For some reason, I ended up in Max's office. I rarely went in there, and I stood in the doorway, recalling all the times I had done the same thing—leaning on the doorframe, telling Max to come for dinner, or to leave his book and join me in the garden. Scold him for working too much.

With a sigh, I went in, sitting in the wingback chair across from his desk. It was where I had always sat when I came in to see him. He would look up from whatever he was working on, his eyes twinkling, his gaze welcoming. His desk would be covered in reference books, files, papers, and notes. Often, his laptop sat on a precarious pile of papers, listing to one side, always in danger of ending up on the floor.

"Hello, my girl," was his standard greeting.

Now, his desk was empty. His laptop shut and set to the side. There were no papers or files—I had spent days sorting and organizing them, sliding them into neat piles and storing them in file boxes. Colin had them since he was fascinated with Max's work, his thoughts on the medical system, and his wealth of knowledge.

I glanced around the room, wondering what had called me here in the middle of the night. I hadn't moved or changed much about this room. It had always been Max's haven, the same way my office had been my own personal space. It was the place we could simply be ourselves and enjoy our own endeavors without the other person.

I drew my knees up to my chest, feeling a wave of emotion. Max was always careful never to stop me from pursuing my own interests. He supported me in everything I chose to do—from working for Bentley, doing some traveling on my own, even the odd hobby I would pick up then discard. He always was there, encouraging and supporting me. Max had been an amazing husband.

A shiver of foreboding went through me. I stared at his desk as three words exploded in my head so clearly, it was as if they were shouted out loud in the room.

You forgot me.

I blinked at the sudden rush of tears, suddenly knowing the reason for my unease and my worry. For the first time since Max died, he hadn't been on my mind. Instead, Jordan had filled my thoughts and overtaken my feelings all weekend—even longer. The only time I'd thought of Max had been in comparison—the things Jordan did that Max hadn't.

How Jordan loved to travel. Enjoyed being on the water. The way he hummed and soothed me in the storm. The passion he had reawakened in me.

Not once during the weekend had I thought of Max or our life together. I allowed Jordan to fill up that place of loneliness and replace it with laughter and joy.

I covered my mouth with my hand as a sob escaped me.

I had compared the two men and found my husband lacking.

How could I have forgotten Max so easily? What kind of wife was I to have moved on so fast?

What had I done?

Betrayed Max. Betrayed our marriage. Had sex with another man. Spent the weekend with him and pushed aside all thoughts of the man I had spent over thirty years with.

A man who was loving, kind, and wonderful. Who gave me a life filled with happiness.

Who deserved to be remembered, not cast aside and forgotten.

It was too soon. I wasn't ready.

And I had to put a stop to this.

JORDAN

I sensed Sandy's withdrawal from me on the flight home. The way she held herself back, the subtle shift when I tried to touch her. As if she no longer wanted to feel my hand on her skin.

She was quiet in the car—tense and anxious. She allowed my embrace before I left, melting into me as if she needed it, and for a moment, I dismissed my notion of worry. She admitted she was tired, so I accepted it. Her pallor could be explained away with fatigue as well, so I convinced myself that was the cause.

But her odd reactions on the phone worried me. The gap I felt between us which had never been there before—even prior to our budding relationship. There had always been an ease between us, but our conversation was stilted and awkward.

I didn't sleep well and went to the office with a heavy heart. Bentley had delayed the usual staff meeting until we returned today. I approached the boardroom apprehensively, unsure as to what I would find. How would Sandy act this morning?

She was in her usual place, already writing in her notebook, Bentley in position at the head of the table. He spoke quickly, and she nodded, keeping up with him as he filled her in on what he required.

He lifted his head as I went by. "Jordan, good morning."

I tilted my chin in acknowledgment. "Bentley." I paused. "Sandy."

She glanced up with a smile. It was her cool, professional one, which I expected, but my chest ached at the signs of a sleepless night. She was paler than yesterday, weariness etched under her eyes.

I sat down, hoping she would look at me, but she kept her eyes focused on the pad in front of her, her hand moving rapidly as Bentley began the meeting. She was still sitting when we filed out.

It bothered me that she never once looked at me, and that even when she spoke, it seemed to me her voice was distant and removed. None of the warmth I associated with Sandy was present.

Twice, I went past her desk, but she wasn't there. I called to ask her about lunch, relaxing a little when she answered, breathless.

"Jordan, I'm sorry. I was in Bentley's office. He is crazy today."

I chuckled. "He must have missed you."

"If the pile of to-do's on my desk is any indication, then yes."

She was swamped, which wasn't a surprise. Bentley relied heavily on her. I was reading too much into this.

"I was wondering about lunch. A sandwich in the park?"

"I can't. Bentley has three meetings this afternoon, and I need to attend all of them. We're leaving in about ten minutes. Rain check?"

"Of course. Maybe tomorrow."

"I'll talk to you later."

She hung up, and my unease returned. She hadn't agreed to lunch tomorrow. She hadn't taken a moment to say anything personal.

I would call her this evening, and we would talk it through. Maybe go see her once I dealt with the real estate agent. Although I hadn't said anything to Sandy, I was on edge about the house and the next steps. I would tell her that as well. I was sure she would listen and help me sort out my feelings.

Perhaps we could address hers as well.

My plan was good—except, I never spoke to Sandy that night. My agent showed up at six, a folder filled with offers, and I spent the next several hours going back and forth with one buyer who was determined to buy the property. By midnight, the deal was done, the papers signed, and I was both elated and relieved. I picked up the phone to call Sandy, then glanced at the clock and hung up.

I stared at the phone. If this had been last week, I was certain I would have called her, regardless of the time. She would have been welcoming and pleased to hear my news, sharing in my happiness of the offer and understanding my relief it was done so quickly. But tonight, I was hesitant because I wasn't sure of her reaction. I worried about disturbing her and afraid if she was dismissive or uncaring of my news that I wasn't sure how I would handle it. I decided to wait until I saw her in the morning.

Once again, my sleep was broken and fragmented.

FIFTEEN

JORDAN

I found her in the kitchen making coffee in the morning. I entered the room, determined to speak to her. She glanced up from pouring water into the coffeemaker.

"Good morning," I greeted her.

"Morning," she replied, pushing the button. "Coffee will be ready in a moment."

"Great, but I didn't come for that."

She leaned against the counter, crossing her arms. She looked casual, but her body was tense. Her tone was cordial, but I preferred it when she spoke to me in that low, breathless voice. "I expected to hear from you last night," she remarked.

I mimicked her stance. "It was past midnight when we finished. I texted you a couple of times, but you didn't respond."

"I was sorting some drawers in Max's office. I forgot my phone in the kitchen."

"I see."

"How did the offers go?"

I sighed and loosened my arms. It felt as if I was talking to a polite stranger, not the woman I spent the weekend with. "I accepted the highest offer. He came in at thirty grand over asking. He wanted a two-week closing, but I got it pushed back to a month. He had no conditions other than the two weeks, so we bartered back and forth for a bit. He was pretty set on it, and I wanted six weeks, but we compromised in the end."

She smiled, a real, genuine Sandy smile. Stepping forward, she laid her hand on my arm. "Jordan, that is wonderful. Congratulations. I'll make sure Bentley knows you need the condo in a month."

I laid my hand over hers, meeting her gaze. What I saw bothered me. Her eyes were dull, and the pain and worry in them made me ache.

"Sandy," I murmured. "Talk to me."

She pulled away. "I am."

I grabbed at her hand, holding it tight. "Something is wrong. I feel it. Talk to me," I repeated.

She didn't try to deny it. "Not here."

"Lunch?"

She paused, then nodded. I felt a flash of relief. If she talked to me, I could help her sort out whatever was going on in her head.

"Okay, I'll pick us up a sandwich."

"All right."

The air around us was tense. Trying to lighten the atmosphere, I lifted my cup. "I'll take that coffee if you're still offering."

Smiling, she held out her hand for my mug. "Of course."

But her eyes remained troubled, and I fought down the feeling that lunch was only going to make things worse.

She waited for me on the bench we often had sat on in the past when we would share lunch. During those earlier days, when we were simply two people drawing comfort from each other. I studied her as I grew close, once again noting her pallor and the anxious set to her shoulders. One of Sandy's greatest gifts had always been that of repose. She rarely fidgeted or squirmed. She didn't play with her hair or drum her fingers restlessly. She was calm, never resorting to theatrics or displays of temper.

Today, her leg swung as she waited, and her fingers drummed on her knee. I knew how high her anxiety was as I approached. I sat beside her, offering her the sandwich and iced tea I had brought her.

"Sorry to have kept you waiting," I said. "The deli was busy."

"I can't go with you to Van's wedding," she blurted out.

I paused in unwrapping my sandwich. That wasn't what I had expected her to say—but it was as good a place to start as anywhere, I supposed. I put the sandwich back in the bag, my appetite gone.

"Can't or won't?"

"Does it matter?"

"To me, yes."

"I can't have people thinking we're a couple. I don't want to disappoint Van, so I will attend, at least for the ceremony, but I'll be going on my own."

Disappointment flooded my chest, but something in her voice made me pause. She sounded regretful, as if the decision caused her pain. I needed her to open up to me. We could work this out together.

I turned to face her fully, ready to battle this out with her. "Odd, I thought we were a couple. You certainly acted that way this past weekend."

"This weekend was wonderful, but it can't happen again."

"I don't understand."

"I'm don't want...*this*." She waved her hand between us, the gesture dismissive and upsetting.

"What are you talking about? We had an amazing time being together. What changed?" I asked, mystified.

"I'm not ready to be a couple again."

"We felt like a couple on the weekend," I repeated. "Very much so." I angled my head to the side, watching her closely, my voice rough as my anger built. Her eyes were blank, the spark I liked so much missing again. "Or is that it, Sandy? We're a couple only when you decide we are? Was this weekend just a little side trip from real life? Scratching an itch, so to speak?"

If possible, her skin became paler—almost a sickly white. "No, it wasn't like that. You know me better than that."

"I thought I did." I cleared my throat. "Then what are you saying?"

"I can't do this, Jordan." She waved her hand back and forth between us again. "I'm not ready. I'm sorry, I thought I was, but I'm not. I can't be in a relationship with you."

My heart plummeted, but I tried to remain calm. "What changed?" I asked again. "You seemed happy this weekend."

"I was—I mean, I thought I was, but then I went home, and I realized that it was a mistake."

"A mistake," I repeated, hating that word.

"Yes. I got caught up."

"In?" I let the word hang, pain lancing through my chest as she kept talking.

"In you. In the possibility of an us."

I wanted to grab her, shake some sense into her, and get her to stop this craziness. "It was more than a possibility. I thought it was a fact."

"No." She shook her head furiously. "I'm not over Max's death yet. I'm not ready to move on."

I didn't want to let her go. I needed to reach her, to make her understand I would be there for her and help her through this. I stretched out my hand to touch her, to let her feel I was right there.

"I know this is hard. I understand—I really do. But, Sandy, my darling girl—"

I didn't get any farther. She jumped to her feet. "Don't call me that!"

I blinked at her vehemence.

"I was 'my girl' to Max—that was his name!"

I held out my hand. "I'm sorry. It slipped out. Sit down and we'll talk this out."

"There is nothing to talk about. I told you I can't do this."

"And I have no say in the matter?"

"No, you don't. You're ready, I'm not. I don't know if I ever will be."

"Don't say that. You have too much love to give. You're too wonderful to live the rest of your life alone."

"I wish people would stop saying that. Stop telling me how to live my life. I do just fine on my own." She almost snarled in her anger. "Max was ill for so long, I had to do everything on my own. So, you don't have to worry about me."

"But I do."

She brushed off her skirt. "I can't do this, Jordan. Not now. I'm sorry if I hurt you. I regret that more than anything else. But I can't be with you when I'm still in love with my husband."

I had to say it. I stood and met her eyes.

"Your husband is dead."

Her eyes grew round and filled with tears. "I know that."

"Yet, you act as if you're betraying him."

"I slept with you."

"Yes, you did. And I slept with you. I thought it was only us in that room, but I guess Max was there as well. Ghosts do that if we let them. Hang around."

"You're a horrible man."

"No, I'm a hurt one. I shouldn't be surprised by this, but I am. I thought you were on the same page I was, but I was obviously wrong. I misjudged what we had. What we felt."

Her shoulders slumped. "I'm sorry. I wish I could express how deeply sorry I am."

"I know you are. I can see it. I wish you could step back and let me help. We could work this through together. Slow down and take our time to—"

"No."

Her voice was firm. She had made up her mind, and I had no choice but to accept her decision.

"Well then, I guess lunch is over. I guess…we're over."

A tear slipped down her cheek. "I'm sorry."

"So you keep saying."

"I don't know what else to say."

"Funny, I never took you for a coward, Sandy."

"What?" she gasped.

"You are. I think you're scared of what you feel for me. I think it frightens you so much that you're using your dead husband as an excuse."

"Go to hell," she seethed.

"Oh, I'm already there."

We glared at each other, our pain bleeding into the air.

She straightened her shoulders and wiped her cheeks. "The office…"

I laughed without humor. "Of course you'd worry about that. Don't think about it. I won't cause you any embarrassment. I'm well aware of who would win that fight. I won't bother you—we'll just go back to being coworkers." I snorted with derision. "I think that will be easier for one of us than the other."

Her muffled sob made me feel horrible. My anger drained away, leaving hurt and pain behind. I gentled my voice.

"Just promise me something, Sandy."

"What?"

"If you change your mind, come and see me. I promise, I'll listen."

Then I bent and kissed her damp cheek.

I wasn't sure whose tears I tasted.

I hurried away before I could find out.

Saturday, I taped up another box, nodding in grim satisfaction. Packing was going well. I had been at it every night this week and all this morning. I had to stay busy. It was the only way I could deal with the hurt and the pain that hit me in waves. I wasn't sleeping much, so I was at the office early and coming home late, wishing at times I had never decided to sell the house.

But there wasn't anything I could do about that now. The fact was, perhaps a new place would be a fresh start in every way now. No memories of Anna or of Sandy would haunt me there.

At least, I told myself that.

I bent to lift another box when the doorbell sounded, and I set it aside to answer the door. A courier waited, handing me a large, flat parcel. My heart fell when I saw it, knowing full well what it was. I signed for it, then carried it to the living room. I set it on the sofa, carefully unwrapped the box and the packing material, and stared at the contents.

It was a print of the painting Sandy had loved at the museum. I had purchased a copy and had it framed and paid extra for fast shipping. I had planned on giving it to her as a surprise, hoping she would want to hang it in my new place and come visit often to see it.

Except now, she wouldn't be coming to my new place, and I wasn't certain she would want this gift, even if I gave it to her in the context of friendship. She'd already given me back the shawl I bought her— still in its wrappings. I'd found it on my desk when I returned to the office from a meeting. I had stared at it, unsure what to do, then simply put it in the trunk of my car and left it there. It was too painful to bring inside.

That odd ache was back in my chest when I woke in the mornings, if I was able to sleep at all. Only this one was new and fresh. Deeper in some ways. Anna had no choice but to leave me. Sandy walked away. I knew I needed to stop thinking about her.

Yet, I couldn't.

We had been cordial and professional the rest of the week after she broke things off with me. As a rule, we didn't often have much inter-action, so if I didn't see her every day, it wasn't out of the ordinary. This week, however, I constantly had papers for Bentley to sign, invoices for Maddox, and reports for Aiden to go over. It felt as if I was in the executive area several times a day.

Sandy was polite, courteous, and removed. She always waved me in or let whatever partner I needed know I was waiting. She offered coffee and a blank smile, her voice carefully neutral.

It broke my heart to see her increasing fragility appear before my eyes. She looked wan and tired. Broken. It reminded me of how she looked after Max died, and once again, there was little I could do to help her since it seemed I was the cause of her altered state. She didn't want my comfort, even though I was desperate to give it to her.

To their credit, none of the boys said a word. They treated me the same, although I saw their worried glances toward Sandy and the confusion in their eyes when they looked at me. I knew I didn't look very good either.

All of us were suffering in silence.

I huffed out a sigh, wondering if I should give the picture away. The sudden rumble of thunder startled me, and I went to the window, lifting the curtain. The skies had darkened as the hours passed, and I'd been busy packing. A storm was coming, the clouds heavy with rain.

I dropped the curtain, feeling the ripple of uncertainty pass through me. Sandy hated storms. Last weekend, I had held her, soothed her during the worst of the squall. How would she make it through the storm today? What would distract her?

I shook my head. It wasn't my business—Sandy made that clear. *She* wasn't my business.

Except, as the thunder rolled, I didn't care. I knew she'd be scared, and I hated that. Hated the fact that she would face it alone, the way she had decided she had to face everything. On her own.

I looked at the picture and made a decision. I wasn't done yet. I had things to say and Sandy was going to hear them.

Determined, I slid the picture back into the box and headed to my car.

I was lucky and found a parking spot two houses down from Sandy's place. The rain had eased off, now just a gentle beat against my window. The thunder was muted and low, but I knew it would build again. According to the weather channel, it would come and go for the rest of the day.

I took advantage of the break and grabbed the box, carrying it up the steps. I entered the porch, the door squeaking in protest as I opened it, and I set down the picture. I knocked on the inner door. Waited. Knocked again. Then I rang the bell. There was no sound from within. I tried the door handle, but it was locked. With a sigh, I gave up—it was obvious Sandy wasn't home. Maybe with the storm approaching, she'd decided to go see Colin. Or Reid. At least she wouldn't be alone. The rain picked up outside, and I decided to leave the picture behind. She would see it when she got home.

I pulled a pen from my pocket and wrote a quick message on the box.

Memories of a wonderful weekend
Think of it with a smile.
Always, Jordan

Maybe it would start a conversation and we could go from there—slowly. She might return it to me. I had no idea, but I hoped she would keep it. I prayed it might spark something in her that made her reach out.

The porch door squeaked again, and I let it slam shut behind me, too tired to worry about it. My head felt heavy as I returned to the car, my footsteps dragging. I slid behind the wheel and let my head fall back, closing my eyes. They burned with unshed emotion.

I had been so sure, so certain of us. That I was ready to move forward, that Sandy was ready. We meshed so well all weekend. Making love to her was akin to being reborn for me. She awakened all my senses, and now it was painful returning to that semi-numbness. Yet without her, I didn't even want to try. I had no desire to date anyone else, build something with a stranger.

Because in the past few days, I accepted the fact that I was in love with Sandy. And the depth of my love wasn't something I could turn off or transfer to someone else. She was the key to my future, but I had perhaps pushed too hard, and now that future was lost.

I wiped my eyes and turned the key, waiting patiently for the windows to clear. Realizing I had caught my coat in the car door, I opened it and tugged the wet hem inside, slamming it shut. I pulled away, driving slowly, noting the thunder ramping up, and the rain coming down harder.

I glanced in my rearview mirror and froze. Behind my car, running and waving her arms, was Sandy. I slammed on the brakes.

What the hell was she doing outside during a storm?

I threw open my door, getting out and turning her way. She was barefoot and dressed in casual clothes, which were wet and clinging to her frame. In the brief moments she'd been outside, her hair had plastered to her head. It was obvious she was crying.

"Sandy," I called out, confused. "What the—"

My words were cut off as she launched herself at me. I caught her to my chest, picking her up off the ground and holding her close. I felt the violent tremors in her body and absorbed her sobs.

I held her tight, unsure of what was happening.

"Don't let go," she begged over and again. "Don't ever let me go."

I held her closer, relief running through my body.

"Never."

SIXTEEN

SANDY

I wrapped my shawl tighter around my shoulders and shivered. The house felt cold today—or maybe it was just me. I had barely slept four hours all week since telling Jordan I couldn't see him anymore.

I couldn't get the devastated look on his face out of my mind. The pain in his eyes. The tears that mingled with mine when he kissed me and walked away.

I was certain I had done the right thing. I wasn't ready.

Except, since breaking it off with Jordan, I couldn't escape the pain I felt. It was as virulent as when Max died, but different. Fresher, more acute somehow. As if my body was telling me I was suffering needlessly.

He called me a coward. At times, I thought perhaps he was right. It scared me to think of moving on, of having feelings for someone again.

Of falling in love and losing him. Experiencing that pain all over again. Knowing I would have to rebuild my life yet again without the person I loved beside me.

It was better to have walked away now.

I wasn't ready.

Even if the look of pain on Jordan's face still haunted me. The hurt in his voice.

I poured the water from the kettle into the cup, letting the tea steep and darken the water. I wrapped my hands around the mug and walked to the living room, switching on the gas fireplace. Outside, the sky was dark, the day foreboding.

I tried not to think of last weekend. Being in Jordan's arms while the storm raged. Feeling safe and calm while he hummed and lulled me to sleep.

Today, I would have to tough it out on my own.

I set aside the tea, not really wanting it. I curled up on the sofa and slipped on some noise-canceling headphones. I would feel better after a nap—I was certain of it. With the low music playing in my head, my body slowly relaxed, and I drifted into sleep.

The sky was dreary and dull. I was lost, wandering in an area I was unfamiliar with. Cold, I pulled on my shawl, shocked to find the ends torn and frayed. I stumbled, gasping as I fell. A pair of strong arms caught me before I hit the pavement, keeping me from injury.

I turned and looked into the face of the man holding me. He smiled, his green eyes warm.

"All right, my darling?"

"Jordan. You're here!"

"Where else would I be?"

"But I sent you away—you were furious with me."

He shook his head. "I was waiting for you. I've been waiting for you for a long time."

"I can't—I told you I can't."

He stood, releasing me. "You can. You need to let him go. He's waiting. We're both waiting for you, Sandy."

"What?"

He indicated behind me with the tilt of his chin. I turned and saw another man standing, watching us. I stepped forward. "Max?"

"Hello, my girl."

"How is this possible?"

"Anything is possible in your dreams."

"Is that what this is?"

"This is anything you want it to be."

"I don't know what to do, Max."

He smiled sadly. "Yes, you do. You need to be the strong woman I know you are. Let me go and find your happiness again."

"I don't know if I can do that."

"You can. It's what I wanted. It's what I always wanted for you. Our chapter is over, Sandy, but you have an entirely new book to write. Grab it. Write it. Live it."

He began to fade. "I'll always be there, Sandy. Just let me be where I belong. In the past."

"Max—no—wait!"

"You don't have to choose. You can love us both. Now, wake up, my girl. Wake up now and grab your happiness. Open the door, Sandy. Open the door!"

And he was gone.

I sat up, gasping. My headphones were on the floor, and outside, the thunder rolled. I heard the rain pelting against the glass, and I ran a shaky hand over my face.

My weird dream played like a movie in my head. It had been so real.

Max's words echoed in my head. The gentle, loving look on Jordan's face danced behind my eyes.

I thought of the other dreams I'd had with Max in them. I always felt, in some way, he was reaching out to me. Guiding me.

Was he guiding me to Jordan? Was that possible?

A noise caught my attention, and I stood. It sounded like the porch door shutting. I scrubbed my face and yawned. I was so tired, and the nap hadn't helped. Slowly, I walked down the hall, assuming a delivery had been left for me. I peeked out the front door, but no one was there. As I suspected, there was a large box off to one side of the porch.

I pulled open the door and looked at the box. There was writing on the side, so I lifted it carefully, carrying it into the house. I read the

145

note from Jordan, tears springing to my eyes. He had been here, no doubt while I was asleep, and brought me something.

I slid the gift from the box, my breath catching, and tears, hot and fast, ran from my eyes. My painting. He'd had a print of it framed for me.

Memories of a lovely weekend.

This painting represented more than a memory.

It was the start of something new and beautiful, and I had thrown it away.

Jordan was right.

I was a coward.

The slam of a car door outside made me lift my head. I hurried to the porch, opening the front door and looking outside. Jordan's charcoal-gray sedan was just pulling away from the curb.

Without a thought, I was outside, running down the street, praying somehow Jordan would see me. I waved my arms, crying his name as loudly as I could, ignoring the cold rain and the thunder that crashed around me.

Suddenly, Jordan's car stopped. He stepped outside, staring at me as I barreled toward him.

"Sandy," he called, "What the—"

I crashed into him, flinging my arms around his neck. I sobbed so hard nothing I was trying to say came out right, but I felt his arms lift me from the ground, holding me close.

"Don't let go," I pleaded. "Don't ever let me go."

"Never," he promised, holding tighter.

Jordan's voice was low in my ear as he set me on my feet. I lifted my head, bewildered when I realized we were on my porch.

"What..."

Jordan shook his head. "You have no shoes on, Sandy. Go inside and change into dry clothes."

I clutched at his hand, feeling frantic. He wasn't going to forgive me. "Don't…please. I'm sorry. Please…you said you'd listen!"

He shook his head, cupping my face between his strong hands. "I have to move my car, my darling. Then I'll come right back, and we'll talk. I'm not going anywhere. I promise."

He looked past me with a chuckle. "If it's still there. I left it running in the middle of the street."

I pushed him. "Go. Quickly."

He opened the porch door, frowning at the squeak. "I need to fix this for you."

"No. That was the sound that woke me. It brought me out to the porch."

"All right, then. It stays."

He hurried down the steps, and despite his assurances, I went to the door and watched as he ran down the street, got in his car, and reversed back into a spot close to the house. He shut off the car and strode back, his steps determined and swift.

I backed up as he came inside.

"Sandy, you're soaking wet and shivering. You need dry clothes." He stroked my cheek. "I'm right here."

"Okay."

Inside, I headed to my room, yanking off the wet clothes and tossing them in the hamper. I pulled on a warm sweater and a pair of yoga pants, then dried my wet hair, pinning it up once I was done. I felt much warmer after I slipped on a pair of fuzzy socks.

I found Jordan in the kitchen, brewing a pot of tea. He eyed me tenderly, holding out his hand. "That's better."

I went to him, letting him draw me close, shutting my eyes as another wave of emotion flooded me. I felt safe with him here. No longer worried or upset, just safe.

And loved.

"Shall we go sit down?" he asked. "We need to talk."

"Yes."

We sat on the sofa. Jordan bent down and picked up my head-phones, lifting his eyebrow in a silent question.

"Noise-canceling headphones. I haven't been sleeping well and I was so tired I thought a nap would help. I put them on to stop hearing the thunder. I must have rolled, and they fell off."

"Then you heard the door squeak?"

I took a sip of my tea. "Not exactly." As simply as I could, I explained my strange dream to Jordan. He listened, not interrupting, then rubbed his face.

"You really think Max was telling you I was here? To go to me?"

"I don't know. Maybe I heard the knocking in my sleep and somehow manifested it into the dream." I shrugged.

He shook his head slowly. "But you think Max was here?"

"I've dreamed of him before," I admitted. I extended my hand, clasping his. "You were right, Jordan. I was being a coward."

"I shouldn't have said that. I was upset." He lifted my hand to his mouth and kissed my fingers. "You're one of the bravest people I know."

"No, I was scared. I felt so much for you and it worried me. I felt disloyal to Max and the years we spent together. As if they meant so little, I could move on and fall in love with someone else so fast. And the thought of loving you—maybe losing you one day—was too much too handle."

Tears formed in my eyes and rolled down my cheeks. "I thought if I stopped it now, then the pain wouldn't be too bad. I didn't think you could mean as much to me as you did. But I was wrong. You were already there in my heart, and it hurt so much."

I lifted my eyes to his, shocked to see tears glimmering in the depths of his green gaze. "You love me, Sandy?"

"Yes."

He moved closer, cupping my cheek. "Good. Because I love you right back."

He leaned his forehead to mine. "I can't tell you the future, my darling. I can only say this. I'm fifty-nine, in good health, and I plan on being around for the next thirty or, god willing, forty years. And I want to spend those with you. If all we had were five days, five weeks, or five months, I would take it."

"Jordan," I sobbed.

"Don't think about the amount of time we have—none of us knows that—think about how we can live it. We can build a life together. A good one. And dream or ghost, Max was right. This is our story now and how we choose to write it. Write it with me, Sandy. Let's fill the pages with memories. Our memories."

I flung my arms around his neck. "Yes."

***

Hours later, I was still curled by his side, his arm holding me close. We talked, cleared the air, both of us expressing our fears and our hopes.

"I would prefer not to have Max popping into the rooms as we talk," he admitted dryly. "That rather freaks me out."

I had to laugh. "It's only the occasional dream." I sighed. "I somehow think he won't be back."

"No?" he asked, grazing my forehead with his lips.

"I think he knows his job is done. He can rest, knowing I'm happy. He always wanted me to be happy."

"I'll do my best."

I rested my head back on his shoulder, peering up at him. "You do make me happy."

"Good."

"Sandy…" His voice trailed off.

"What?"

"As soon as you're ready, I want you to sell this house and come live with me in the condo."

I sat up, shocked. "That's moving a bit fast, isn't it?"

I shrugged. "Well, as you pointed out earlier, we aren't getting any younger. In the meantime, we can furnish it together, making it ours. When you're ready, you can move in." He winked. "Hopefully, if I do my job right, soon."

"How would your kids feel about that?"

He pursed his lips. "I think they would want me to be happy. Gina and Warren are coming soon for a week to help me sort some things and take what they want from the house and what's in the warehouse. You can meet them, and we'll take it from there."

"Have it all planned out, do you?"

He grinned. "That's my job, you know. I organize and facilitate. Bentley calls me an expert."

"Yes, he does."

"Think about it, Sandy. That's all I'm asking."

"Yes."

"Yes, you'll think about it, or yes, you'll move in?"

"Both? I just need a little time, Jordan."

He kissed me. Slowly and sweetly—I felt his adoration and love in that kiss.

"I love you," he murmured.

It felt so good to hear those words, and to say them back.

"I love you too, Jordan."

He was smiling as he kissed me again.

SEVENTEEN

SANDY

The music swelled, and everyone chuckled as Van left his spot at the altar, walked down the aisle, and met Liv partway. He kissed her and they walked up the aisle together, with him holding her daughter Samantha—or Mouse, as Van called her—close, and holding Liv's hand.

Their vows were simple, the ceremony short, no doubt in order to make sure Mouse didn't get bored and wander off. Van had already bribed her with new sparkly shoes once to get her up the aisle.

I smiled through my tears. They were happy ones, not sad. My smile became wider as a handkerchief was tucked into my hand and Jordan drew me closer. I dabbed at my eyes and dared to glance at him. He was extraordinarily fond of Van and thought of him much like a son. They were good friends, and I knew how excited he was that Van had found a woman as wonderful as Liv. She was perfect for him. Van adored Sammy, and she returned his feelings tenfold. They made a lovely little family.

Jordan was smiling, despite his glistening eyes. I loved the fact that he showed and shared his emotions. He turned his head, meeting my gaze. He lifted his hand and traced one finger down my cheek with an indulgent smile and tilted his head slightly toward the altar. Our eyes held a silent conversation.

That is going to be us—soon.

Slow your roll, Jordan.

Can't, woman. No time to waste.

I tried not to laugh. As I was discovering, although he had the patience of a saint at work and was known for his meticulous ways, in his personal life, he tended to be more—*impatient.*

Since he'd shown up at my door on Saturday, I had lost count of the number of "dates" we had actually had. Aside from the office, and our nights, we were together. Lunches were shared in the park daily. Stolen kisses in the kitchen at the office. Flowers, chocolates, and my favorite pastries appeared by my keyboard. Sweet texts arrived at different moments of the day, always making me smile. Every evening, he appeared at my desk.

"Ready to go, my darling?" he would murmur. I would take his hand, and our evening would begin.

A couple of nights, I went to his house, helping him pack and sort. Anna obviously had exquisite taste, and I helped Jordan pick some pieces to go to his new place. A few nights, he came to my place and we cooked dinner, working well together in the kitchen. He was a great cook, especially his seafood pasta—which I loved so much, I made him promise to make me every week.

But when the evening was over, we separated. I knew Jordan wasn't comfortable in Max's house, and I didn't want to share a bed in the same room he'd shared with Anna. I had no problem cuddling on the sofa, sharing long, passionate kisses in my kitchen, but there was a line there neither of us wanted to cross.

Which was why, Jordan informed me yesterday, he had booked us a hotel room for the night.

"There is no way I can hold you close, dance with you, then drop you off at home," he informed me when I asked why. *"I've been patient, my darling. You can only ask a man to take so much."*

I had held in my amusement, because frankly, I was feeling the same way.

This afternoon when he picked me up, he had stood back, sweeping his gaze over me head to toe in a long, lazy glance. Then he shook his head.

"Thank god."

"I'm sorry?" I asked.

"Thank god I booked that hotel room. You look like a million bucks." He ran a hand over his face. "I hope there is dancing. I want to see you move in that sexy number."

I tried not to blush but failed. Jordan had that effect on me. I had bought another new dress—this one in a deep emerald-green color, with layers of beads that reminded me of a flapper dress from the twenties. It was held up with slender straps on my shoulders and barely skimmed my knees. It shimmered and danced when I moved, the beads almost musical as they bounced and swayed. I had my hair up, showing off my neck and shoulders, which, thank god, were still firm, the skin taut. I carried the lovely shawl Jordan had bought me in Boston.

From the look on Jordan's face and the force of his kiss, I had a feeling he was looking forward to seeing the dress on the floor of the hotel room.

After the dancing.

He'd been close all afternoon, tucking me to his side, running his fingers over my bare shoulder, dropping a kiss to my skin on occasion. We laughed and enjoyed the outpouring of love that surrounded the event.

I danced with all my boys, each of them trying to outdo the other. Maddox was his usual suave, graceful self on the dance floor. Aiden spun me around to a fast number, gyrating his hips and making me laugh as Cami shook her head at his antics. Van and Halton were both solicitous partners. Reid made my heart ache with his awkward, sweet, fumbling attempt at a waltz. He kept apologizing, and he seemed grateful when Bentley stepped in, tapping him on the shoulder firmly.

"My turn—before you injure her."

I smiled as we moved, Bentley's footwork perfect, his leading confident. He was an excellent dancer. He peered down at me. "You're happy."

It was a statement, not a question.

"Very."

"Jordan can't keep his eyes off of you."

I glanced over his shoulder, looking at Jordan. He sat with the family I had created, at ease and smiling. He was talking to Reid, leaning forward, his arms resting on his thighs. He was nodding and listening to whatever Reid was saying, but his gaze was focused on me. Intent and dark with longing. His lips curled into a smile when he saw me watching him, and he threw me a subtle wink.

I felt my blush creep up my neck, and I cursed under my breath. "Damn that man, he does this to me all the time."

Bentley grinned, swinging me around. "It's good to see."

I met his blue gaze. He was relaxed and happy—a changed man from the one I had worried would never allow himself to feel for another person.

"I've fallen in love with him, Bentley," I confessed.

He cocked his head. "I can see that."

"How do you feel about that?" I asked.

He twirled me again. "I think the question is, how do you feel about it?"

"I feel good."

"It shows." His grip on my waist tightened. "That's all I—we—want for you, Sandy. For you to be happy."

"I spoke to Aaron this week. He called me."

"And he said...?" Bentley let the question trail away, watching me closely. He knew I was close with Max's son. Our friendship had been strong all through my relationship with his father.

I smiled, recalling Aaron's words.

"Colin tells me you're seeing someone."

"Oh, ah, yes, I am," I replied, the worry evident in my voice.

"Why did I hear it from him, Sandy?"

"I wasn't sure how to tell you. How you would react," I confessed.

He chuckled. "You dating again? I'm thrilled. You should be living and enjoying, Sandy." His voice became teasing. "Is he younger? Finally got your boy toy?"

"No, my age." I swallowed. "It's Jordan Hayes from the office."

"Ah, great guy. Dad liked him."

"Yes. I—I like him as well."

"I figured." Then he paused dramatically. "Jeez—I'm not gonna have to

*call him Dad, am I? It was hard enough to explain a stepmom my age, never
mind if I have to face that too," he teased.*

I laughed with him. "I think Jordan will do."

*"Whew. I'm coming down in a few weeks to meet him. Give him the
gears."*

"I'll warn him."

"You do that."

"He was fine. He's coming to meet Jordan. 'Give him the gears,' I
think he said."

"Jordan's up to the task. I have no worries." Bentley smirked,
leading me in a twirl.

"I think so too. Jordan looks forward to meeting him."

Bentley winked. "Then things are progressing well. I'm pleased."

A hand appeared, tapping Bentley on the shoulder. "Sorry to cut
in, Bentley, but all you boys have stolen my woman long enough,"
Jordan stated.

Bentley chuckled, good-natured. "I supposed we have had her long
enough. We have to share."

The meaning behind his words was obvious. Jordan smiled. "Yeah,
you have. I've got it from here."

Bentley leaned down and kissed my cheek. He placed my hand in
Jordan's and clapped him on the shoulder. "Yes, I think you do."

T he hotel room was spacious and comfortable. We barely made
it in the door before Jordan had me in his arms, heading for the
bed. I laughed as I clung to his shoulders. He made me feel special—
safe and protected.

He set me beside the bed, turning me around and unzipping my
dress. He followed the path of the zipper with his lips, kissing down
my spine.

"Jesus, you're naked under here," he groaned and spun me around,
hooking the thin straps down my arms. "Shimmy for me one more
time tonight, Sandy."

I did as he requested, the sparkling dress glittering at my feet.

My grin matched his. "Lose the suit."

In seconds, he was naked, his well-tailored clothes tossed behind him.

"I want to have you with those shoes on, my darling," he breathed out.

"You can have me any way you want me."

He groaned and sank to his knees. He tugged off one shoe, then the other, both of them added to the pile behind him, carelessly discarded. "Later," he promised, kissing his way up my leg.

I shivered as he stroked his hands up, smoothing them over the backs of my thighs, pulling me flush to his mouth, kissing my center. "Right now, I need you. All of you."

He cupped my ass, stroking and kneading. "I hope you don't expect to get much sleep tonight."

Peering down, I smiled. "No."

He stood, tossing me on the bed as if I weighed nothing. He crawled up the mattress, hovering over me. "Good."

I pulled him down to my mouth. "Yes, it is."

With a low groan, he kissed me.

And I was lost.

I sighed in contentment, curled up against Jordan's shoulder. He brushed his hand up and down my arm in long, gentle passes. I felt his breath stir my hair, the warmth of his skin under my cheek, and the strength of his muscles under my fingers.

"All right, my darling?"

I peeked up at him. "More than all right."

"You were wonderful."

I chuckled, running my fingers over his chest. "You were rather spectacular yourself."

I felt his smile against my head. "We're spectacular together."

I hummed in agreement. The room was quiet for a few moments, both of us basking in the warmth of the moment.

"Your feet still sore?"

I wiggled my toes. "A little. I danced a lot, and those heels were high."

"Those heels were sexy. So was that damn dress. They were made for you to dance in." He chuckled low in his chest. "And for me to look at you while you did."

"I'm glad you liked them."

He pulled me closer. "I like how you feel in my arms, Sandy. We should go dancing more. There are a couple of clubs with special dance nights for waltzing and the like. Would you like to go?"

The thought of dancing with Jordan thrilled me. He was an excellent dancer—as confident as Bentley, but with more experience. He had proved to be an excellent partner tonight, surprising me with his moves.

"Yes."

"Excellent. I'll look into it."

"Van looked very happy."

"I think he is. Liv suits him—and he adores her and Mouse."

"I agree."

Quiet stretched again for a moment. "Do you see that for us one day, Sandy?"

I wasn't surprised by the question. I had seen it lurking in his eyes all day.

"I would like to think so. One day."

"In the not too distant future."

I patted his chest. "How about we see how it goes when I meet Gina and Warren tomorrow and the next little while settles for us? You might change your mind."

I gasped as he rolled, hovering over me. "Not a chance. I see the next phase of my life, Sandy. A new place. More traveling. Dancing. Time on the boat. All with you."

I traced my finger down his cheek.

"My kids will like you. Given time, I think they will love you. They want me happy, and you do that for me. I have no worries about their acceptance of us."

"I hope you're right."

"I am. Tomorrow is going to be fine, and the next chapter in my life is going to be great. As long as you're with me, it will be." He pressed a kiss to my mouth. "So, are you? Are you with me, Sandy?"

I met his warm green gaze. I could see it all. The next years unfolding, our lives entwining. It wouldn't always be easy, but I knew with Jordan, it would be worth it. He was right. Everyone was right. I deserved to be happy.

"I'm with you. I love you," I whispered.

A smile broke out on his face and he kissed me. It was a kiss of new beginnings, promises made, and a future that was bright. "Thank you." He kissed me again. "I love you, my darling."

His words filled my chest with happiness. "Then let's start living, Jordan."

He touched his forehead to mine.

"I'm with you."

The next day, I waited at the house, nervous. I had been unsure about meeting Jordan's children in the home he shared with his wife, but in the end, we agreed it was best to meet them where they would be comfortable. Jordan had gone to pick them up, and I stayed behind to prepare a light lunch. He had texted to say they would arrive soon.

I laid out the sandwiches and switched on the coffee. It felt a little odd to be in his kitchen, but not uncomfortable. It looked very different with so many things gone. I didn't feel as if I was intruding in Anna's space, especially since Jordan had told me that he had used the kitchen more than she did. He enjoyed cooking more than Anna had.

I heard the sound of the car arriving, the doors opening, and footsteps coming up the steps. I wiped my hands on my slacks and touched my hair, making sure it was in place. I wanted, at least, to make a good first impression.

Jordan walked in, followed by Gina and Warren. Jordan smiled at me, setting down the suitcases and shrugging off his coat. He kissed my cheek, murmuring in my ear. "It's fine, my darling. Relax."

Then he turned and made the introductions. "Gina and Warren, this is Sandy. Sandy, these are my children."

I smiled and held out my hand, hoping it wasn't shaking. Gina looked like Anna, slender with light brown hair and brown eyes. Her expression was warm and open, and she ignored my hand and gave me a hug.

"Lovely to meet you," she said.

Warren was cooler, his handshake firm as he nodded and stepped back. "Sandy."

I smiled, not surprised. Jordan had warned me Warren might be more reticent.

"He took Anna's death hard," he explained to me. "He isn't upset about me moving on, he's just not..." His voice trailed off.

"Thrilled," I finished for him.

He lifted one shoulder. "My son has trouble forming attachments. He was especially close to Anna. Give him a little time—he'll warm up."

Warren stood beside Jordan, a younger version, with the same build and eye color. He wasn't unfriendly, but I could sense his apprehension. There was nothing I could do to help him, except allow him to get to know me and come to terms with the relationship Jordan and I had. I had no plans on letting Jordan go. I only hoped Warren would warm to me.

"I have a late lunch ready," I offered. "You must be tired."

Gina wrapped her arm around mine as we walked to the kitchen. "Dad is going to take us and show us the condo later."

"It's lovely. I think your father will be happy there."

She squeezed my arm, her voice low. "I think he's happy now."

I laughed, liking her very much. There was a warmth to her that reminded me of Jordan. An openness in her expression and manner. I recalled Anna being more reserved, which meant Warren probably took after her. She was always kind and friendly, but she held herself back, unlike Jordan who seemed to encompass everyone around him with his friendliness. I would let Warren warm up in his own time.

"I'm glad you think so," I responded.

"Warren will come around."

I side-eyed her, trying not to laugh at her wink.

"My brother is a bit slower, but he'll get there. I think you're good for my dad. He'll see that."

I reached for the coffee. "I hope so."

Lunch helped. Warren relaxed and asked me a lot of questions. He was fascinated with BAM and the work they did.

"Dad always talks about them. They treat him very well."

"They treat everyone well."

"They're huge in the land market. Real estate development. Their company is associated with excellence even out in Alberta."

I nodded. They had various dealings in other provinces, although Bentley preferred to stay close to home. "I am very proud to work for them."

"As am I," Jordan offered.

"And you look after all of them?" Warren asked.

I laughed. "In a manner of speaking, yes."

Jordan spoke up. "Bentley often says Sandy is the glue that holds the place together." He smiled at me indulgently. "I would have to agree." He lowered his voice. "She looks after me very well."

Warren studied us wordlessly, then smiled, looking very much like Jordan. His voice was surprisingly light and teasing when he spoke.

"Spoken like a man in love, Dad."

Jordan smiled so widely, his eyes crinkled. He reached over and squeezed my hand. "I suppose I am."

Warren laughed, taking a sip of his coffee. Gina winked at me, as if to say, "*Told you so*."

I was so flustered, I blushed. Jordan laughed and kissed my hand.

I stood. "I should go and let you get at it."

I was surprised and shocked when both Warren and Gina shook their heads. "Stay," Gina urged.

"Many hands, light work, Dad always says," Warren stated. "Besides, we want to get to know you."

And right then, I knew it would be okay.

"I would love to."

Jordan smiled, his gaze taking us all in.

"Perfect."

EPILOGUE

THE FOLLOWING JUNE

SANDY

The sun glinted, catching the light on the water outside the window. The day was lovely, warm, and perfect. I shut my eyes again and focused on the soothing sound of Chopin playing through the speakers. In the background, I heard the murmurings of happiness from my girls as they waited for me to finish. My stomach was full of butterflies—both nervous and excited.

"Almost done," Cami assured me.

I laughed. "It's fine. We have plenty of time."

Becca placed another glass of champagne on the table beside me. "We have another bottle, too."

I smiled. "It's delicious."

Emmy laughed from her spot on the sofa. "Bentley sent it. Only the best for his Sandy."

Cami came around in front of me, tucking in a strand of my hair, patting another part.

She spun my chair, so I faced the mirror. "I think we're done."

I gasped as I took in the elaborate style she had made with my hair. A beautiful French braid, intricately laced with deep green ribbons to match my sash, with glittering beads and glossy pearls tucked into the braid. Tiny speckles of glitter shone under the lights, highlighting the white of my hair. Perfectly placed tendrils touched my neck.

I clasped her hand. "Cami, it's perfect."

She beamed at me, suiting the pet name Aiden had given her of "his Sunshine." When she smiled, it was as if the sunshine had emerged from behind a cloud, brightening everything around her.

"I'm glad you like it."

All my girls gathered around me. I looked at their youthful beauty reflected in the mirror. Emmy's unique bohemian looks, Cami's striking coloring, Dee's sedate prettiness—all different and all lovely. Becca was the girl next door, appealing and sweet. Liv was curvy and warm with her golden hair and lovely eyes. Katy had become another one of my girls, and she was a classic beauty with her dark hair and vivid blue eyes.

And the best part, they were all equally as beautiful inside.

Cami lifted her phone. "Group selfie!"

We pressed close, and she snapped several pictures of us all.

I lifted my glass. "To my girls. Thank you for being with me today."

They all lifted their glasses, sipped, and moved to the various sofas placed in the room. Standing, I reached into my bag and began handing them each a small box.

"My gift to you. I know you are all sitting for the ceremony, but I consider you all my attendants."

I laughed at their eagerness to open their gifts. Each girl wore a shade of green—they ranged from a soft mint to a rich, warm forest— each suiting the wearer. Cami had designed all their dresses, and mine, and their husbands all wore ties to match. They would be in all the family photos, because the bottom line was—they were my family.

Their squeals of delight made me smile. I'd given them each a necklace, designed for them, by the same woman who had designed my ring. The necklace was an infinity symbol and contained a diamond and an emerald to represent today and engraved with the date. The boys were each getting a set of cuff links from Jordan in the same design. It was our gift to them.

There were hugs, some tears, and lots of laughs as I helped fasten the necklaces around their necks.

"You are all so beautiful," I said, holding my hands in front of me. "All my girls."

That prompted another round of hugs.

Wiping her eyes, Cami clapped her hands. "Time to get you into your dress!"

I slipped behind the screen, and Cami helped me step into the dress, fastening the hidden zipper, fluffing the skirt, and ensuring the sash was perfect.

I stood and looked in the mirror, eyeing myself critically. Cami had done a wonderful job. My dress was a soft silver-gray lace, straight at the neck and ending at the knee. It was cinched in at the waist with a deep green sash that matched my pretty shoes. The back was a deep cowl, the lace shimmering as it gathered low off my shoulders, showing off my neck and the line of my spine. It was daring, sexy, and I felt like a million bucks in it. Jordan would love it. He told me often enough how much he loved my long legs. He also enjoyed kissing his way down my spine. The dress might drive him to distraction.

I grinned at my reflection. Perfect.

I stepped out, pleased at the girls' reactions.

"Oh Sandy!" Emmy clasped her hands at her chest. "That dress—Cami! It's gorgeous!"

"You're beautiful," Dee whispered.

Liv grinned. "What a knockout."

"Reid is going to cry."

"So is Richard. He is such a sap at weddings."

Cami dabbed her eyes. "Jordan is going to drag you away and have his wicked way with you. I outdid myself."

There was a knock on the door, and I turned my head. "Come in."

Gina entered, carrying a box. She stopped when she saw me. "Oh, Sandy, you are stunning!"

I twirled and she laughed. "My dad is gonna go crazy!"

I smiled at the woman I considered both an adopted daughter and my friend. Jordan had been correct. We became friends the day we met, and our bond had only grown stronger. She was accepting and gracious about my relationship with Jordan, pleased to see her father happy. Warren had taken a while to warm up to me. He had been polite but cool when we met, but seeing me with his father, he had accepted me, and we'd grown closer They both called me Sandy, but I was Nan to Gina's children.

"You look beautiful yourself."

She wore a green dress as well, although hers was loose and flowy. No one had been more surprised than she was to discover she was pregnant a few months ago. Now at six months, she was well rounded. She was also exhausted and had begged off the earlier luncheon with the girls.

She chuckled as she set down the flowers. "I feel fat."

She greeted the girls, exchanging hugs. I had already given her the necklace last night, and it sparkled at her throat.

"You are pregnant, not fat. And you're glowing."

She smiled, rubbing her hand along the swell of her stomach. "I'm in good company today."

I had to laugh. There were a few pregnant guests today. My boys and their families were all growing. I knew about Emmy, but I had noticed another guest only sipping at her champagne, not really drinking it. I didn't say anything, knowing it was her news to share when she was ready.

I sat down, reaching for my shoes. I held one up, admiring the touch of sparkle on the strap and toes. They were a deep green, matching the sash at my waist and the ribbons woven into my hair.

I looked in the mirror, pleased with what I saw. I turned my head side to side, admiring the intricate braiding. I reached for my earrings, but Gina's voice stopped me. "Dad asked me to give you this."

I turned, looking at the small box she offered me. I accepted it, unfolding the small note that was attached.

The sky is blue, the venue borrowed,
The day is perfect, and I am old.
Now, in this box, if I may be so bold,
Is your something new.
I may suck at poetry,
But I ask that you do
Marry me today, my darling.
Jordan.

I opened the lid, smiling and crying at the same time. Jordan always made me laugh with his humor.

Nestled in ivory satin was a set of lovely emerald earrings. Elegant and beautiful, they matched the design of my engagement ring. I hadn't wanted a ring, thinking I was too old to be "engaged," but Jordan had surprised me with this ring one day. A classic emerald cut stone, with smaller emeralds and diamonds on the band, it was exquisite. Our wedding bands echoed the design, and now I had earrings to match.

I met the girls' curious stares and showed the earrings to them.

"They are lovely," Gina enthused. "I always wondered, why emeralds?"

"They remind me of your father's eyes," I admitted. "I never had a favorite stone before."

She threw her arms around me. "I am so glad he has you."

I hugged her back. "Thank you."

She pulled away, grinning. "I think your grandbaby is happy too."

I laughed, laying my hand on her stomach, feeling the pushing of a foot or a hand. I was excited about this baby—about all the babies. Jordan and I would be surrounded by little ones for years to come.

There was another knock, and Colin came in, stopping when he saw me.

"Nan," he breathed out. "You are gorgeous."

"You clean up pretty well yourself."

"Everyone is here, the boys are in their places, the chaplain is ready, and Jordan is anxious." He lifted one eyebrow. "What about you?"

With a final glance in the mirror, I picked up my bouquet and the extra roses I had requested.

"Ready."

The girls stood. "That's our cue," Emmy said. There was a flurry of hugs, kisses, and a few tears, then they left.

Gina smiled. "I'll see you at the altar."

She would stand beside me, and Warren would be beside Jordan. We were keeping that part simple.

I turned to Colin. He grinned and tugged his sleeves, showing me his cuff links. "We all loved them."

"Good."

He stepped forward. "I want today to be perfect for you, Nan. I want you to be happy."

"I am," I assured him. "And today has already been amazing. Now, I get to marry Jordan, so it will be perfect."

He kissed my cheek, then crooked his arm. "Let's do this."

The music played softly, the small gathering in front of me all friends and people I considered family. We were getting married in a beautiful ballroom where we often danced on the weekends. Situated by the waterfront, it was romantic and beautiful, with huge crystal chandeliers that glittered and sparkled in the sunset. The wooden floor was polished to a high gloss and the walls draped in yards of gleaming satin. It was set up for the ceremony on one side, and after we were married, we had space for a catered dinner and dancing on the other end. It was elegant, simple, and everything we wanted for our day.

Then I had a surprise for Jordan waiting.

The aisle was wide, a thick runner under my feet, and strewn with flowers. There were seven rows of chairs and on the left-hand side of each row were the men I thought of as my sons.

They had all wanted to give me away, even calling me into the boardroom to present their arguments.

Bentley's was short and succinct. "She was mine, first."

Maddox insisted he would be the best dressed for the occasion.

Aiden had a PowerPoint ready, which mysteriously failed to work.

Reid never got to give his thoughts since Aiden chased him out of the office, yelling that he'd been sabotaged. All Reid managed to get out was "She loves me best!"

Richard sent a text.

It should be me, just so you don't have to choose between the BAM boys.

Van laughed, sipping his coffee. "I just wanted to see this spectacle, Sandy. Carry on."

Once I stopped laughing and got Reid out of the headlock Aiden had him in, I explained it would be Colin, but shared my idea for the day, and they were all fine.

Each man stood in the aisle, tall and handsome, waiting for me to pass. It was the longest, most emotional walk down the aisle I could have asked for. Van, Richard, Reid, Maddox, Aiden, and finally, Bentley were all demonstrative, the gruff and stern businessmen fading away and the loving, wonderful men they were inside, present and waiting. As they bent for a kiss and a quiet word, I gave them a rose and told them why they were so special to me.

Bentley—his leadership and loyalty to those he loved.

Aiden—his strength and the protectiveness to the people he called family.

Maddox—his wisdom and sense of humor.

Van—his innate goodness and the depth of his love for his family

Richard—for the bond he had with my boys and the tenacity he possessed.

Finally I got to Reid. I could barely speak as I met his eyes. I leaned forward and kissed his cheek, whispering three words, "My favorite son."

He kissed me back, tears in his eyes. "My mother."

They all made sure I saw their cuff links, all eager to make me smile. Each of them was extraordinary to me in a different way, and I loved them all dearly. I was grateful for waterproof mascara as I made my way toward Jordan, who waited patiently, tears glimmering in his eyes as he watched me with the boys.

Finally, we reached the front row, and Colin wrapped me in his arms and kissed my forehead before he took his place at the end of the row. "I love you, Nan."

I pressed my final rose into his palm. "I love you."

I swept my gaze across the small gathering. All my boys sat with their wives, their hands clasped together, the love and happiness for me evident on their faces. Aaron beamed at me from his place, sitting beside Jennifer and Colin. Jennifer had only arrived today, coming straight from the airport, so she'd declined to be part of the ceremony, electing to sit with her dad and brother. But her smile was wide and open, and I knew she was happy for me. Around her throat was the necklace I had given her, and Aaron had a rose pinned to his lapel and cuff links in his sleeves.

I turned to face Jordan, who held out his hand. I slipped mine into his and we moved forward together, one final step in our journey toward each other. His grip was warm and sure, the look in his eyes leaving me no doubt of his love. I inhaled deeply, a sense of peace and wonder filling my body.

"Dearly beloved..."

Bentley stood, tapping the side of his glass. We had kept things informal, very little in the way of speeches. Jordan and I had thanked everyone for coming, and there had been the usual lifting of glasses and brief moments of seriousness, but other than that, it was casual.

I looked at Jordan, confused. He bent close. "He asked, my darling. They all did. I couldn't refuse."

169

I sighed and sat back, even more confused when Aiden, Maddox, and Reid all stood as well.

Bentley tugged his sleeves, then met my eyes.

"Good evening. My name is Bentley Ridge." He indicated the small group around him. "These are my business partners." He was formal as he introduced each of the men standing beside him. I tried not to laugh since I was certain everyone in the room knew who they were.

Bentley cleared his throat. "Sandy works for my company. Technically, I am her boss."

"Except we all know who runs the place." Aiden leaned in with a wide grin as he spoke into the microphone.

Everyone laughed, including me. Bentley elbowed Aiden out of the way. "Move it, Tree Trunk. I'm talking."

"You always are," Aiden shot back.

Bentley rolled his eyes. "As I was saying, Sandy works at my company, but she is so much more to me—*to us*—than an employee." His voice lost its cool tone, instantly warming. "She is our family."

I felt the tears begin. Jordan pulled me close, wrapping his arm around my shoulder. He pressed a kiss to my head. "Steady, my darling. I don't think you're going to make it, otherwise."

"Sandy met me, Aiden, and Maddox many years ago—"

Aiden interrupted again. "Don't worry, Sandy, we won't say how many years."

A chuckle erupted from my lips, and I shook my head in amusement, grateful for the reprieve.

Bentley rolled his eyes and continued.

"As I recall, we were having a debate about how to do the laundry properly. Apparently, none of us got it right, and Sandy slipped through the bushes to correct us." He smiled at me. "Since then, she has charted our course, guiding us through a lot of rough waters." He winked. "That one was for you, Jordan."

Jordan laughed and waved. "Got, it, Bentley."

Bentley became serious. "At BAM, we hold family dearer than anything. And none are as dear to all of us as Sandy is." He looked at Jordan. "We wish you all the best. Nothing but smooth sailing and sunny skies." He held up his finger. "We are entrusting the woman we all consider our adoptive mother to you, Jordan. Take great care of her, as she means the world to us."

I heard Jordan catch his breath, and he nodded. Tears threatened again for me.

"You have always been part of our family, Jordan, but now those bonds are even tighter. Welcome to the BAM clan. I suppose if Sandy is the matriarch, you are now the patriarch."

Aiden leaned in, once again providing comic relief. "I'd like to discuss my allowance."

The room broke into laughter again.

Maddox stepped forward, pushing Aiden out of the way. "We know Sandy well and thought we would share a few of our insights with you. Since you're a newly married man, we thought you could benefit from our experience."

"Oh boy," I muttered, knowing the serious part of the speech was done.

Jordan threw back his head in laughter. "I'm listening, boys."

"Never tell her what to do. Let her think it's her idea. It's best that way," Maddox deadpanned.

"Because it usually is," I called.

"She hates lettuce on any hot sandwich," Aiden advised. "She gets really ornery about it."

"I'll remember that," Jordan assured him.

Bentley grinned. "Never try to sneak in the lights with the whites. You do not want to have to listen to that lecture. My ears burned for days."

Jordan nodded sagely.

"Always make sure she has coffee before asking her to make a decision."

"For the love of god, don't put cream in her tea," Reid instructed.

"If she asks you about a dress, a blouse anything—the answer is perfect. You look perfect."

The boys went on, making everyone laugh—especially Jordan. As we'd lived together for a while, he already had discovered all these things about me, but I knew the boys wanted to make me smile.

Bentley took control again. "I think we've covered it all, except this."

Richard and Van joined the boys, a solid wall of men staring at Jordan, no doubt trying to intimidate him.

Bentley met my gaze across the tables with a subtle wink. "Sandy is a queen to us. Treat her that way. Or you'll answer to us. All of us."

The guys all flexed, and I had to smother my laughter.

Aiden finished it off. "We know how to get blood out of a carpet. Sandy taught us."

Jordan's shoulders shook with mirth.

"Of course she did."

"Happy, my darling?" Jordan's voice murmured in my ear.

"Very much so," I responded.

"Quite the speech from your boys."

"I hope you're scared."

"Frightfully so."

"Good. Such sage advice for the newly married man."

We both chuckled.

The boys had followed up their "speech" with hugs, laughter, and a lot of back slaps.

"Have I told you how exquisitely beautiful you are?"

"Not in the past ten minutes, no."

"Remiss of me. Your beauty eclipses the sun today, Sandy." He chuckled, running his fingers over my cheek. "There's the color I love."

I shook my head, pretending to be exasperated, while secretly thrilled. He could still make me blush. I hoped that never changed.

After our brief but emotional ceremony, we'd had pictures taken while our guests sipped champagne and nibbled on canapés. There had been many "family" pictures. Of us with Jordan's children and grandchildren. Colin, Jennifer, and Aaron. My boys, their families, large group shots. All of which I planned to put on the walls in the condo.

I had moved in with Jordan a few months ago. Aiden teased me mercilessly about living in sin and demanding Jordan make an honest woman of me whenever he could. Reid gave him a hard time as well, and Jordan took it all in stride with his usual good humor. He surprised me with a proposal on Valentine's Day and the request we get married soon. He kept the ring as another surprise, extending our celebrations for days.

I gave Colin the house the way Max and I had planned. He had been grateful and excited, surprising me when he asked if he could keep some of the furniture. He kept Max's den exactly the way it was, and after adding some pieces of his own, made it into his place. He was still seeing the pretty nurse he had brought to meet me. Miranda was lovely and suited Colin well. She understood his drive and dedication, her own personality much the same. I was certain they would be living in the house together before long.

"Are your feet sore?" he asked, drawing me closer.

I had danced all evening. All my boys, and Jordan, kept me on the floor. Even Reid had practiced and moved me around with far greater ease than at Van's wedding.

"A little. I added an extra gel cushion on the bottom, so not as bad as last time."

"Good plan. I don't want you sore." He lowered his mouth to my ear. "At least not yet. That dress is driving me crazy, my darling. I can hardly wait to get it off of you."

I shivered, loving the deep tone to his voice. Jordan was a passionate lover, and I looked forward to being alone with him soon and seeing exactly how much he liked my dress.

He lifted our hands which were clasped together on his chest and kissed my knuckles. "Am I going to find out your surprise soon, my darling? It's highly unusual for the groom not to plan the honeymoon. I'm getting more curious every moment."

"Soon." I grinned.

"What are you up to?"

"I want to enjoy every moment of tonight with our loved ones. Then the next two weeks you are mine. Utterly mine. Only us —alone."

He pulled me closer. "I love the sound of that, but I'm going to go mad with speculation. You didn't even allow me to pack a suitcase. One suit and a bag of toiletries isn't much for two weeks."

I hid my grin by laying my head against his shoulder. I had bought him everything he would need, and it was already waiting for him. My things were there as well. I had planned this honeymoon out to the last detail. Jordan had been surprised when I'd informed him that I was taking care of the honeymoon, but he'd finally agreed when he saw how much it meant to me.

Colin, Bentley, and Van had helped me. Especially Bentley, who, after I talked to him about my idea, became very interested in the concept and purchased the item I required to make Jordan's dream come true. Bentley decided it was an excellent investment and BAM would get a great deal of use from it. I knew it was useless to argue with him.

"You'll know soon," I repeated.

Jordan sighed, his breath warm on my forehead. "All right, my darling. Keep torturing me."

I tilted up my head, meeting his gaze. "That's what wives are for."

He covered my mouth with his.

"Yes, they are." He smiled against my lips.

———

Hours later, we arrived at the marina. Jordan slipped from the limo, looking confused but holding out his hand to help me from the car. I tugged his hand, excitement coursing through my body as I led him toward the dock.

He laughed, the sound uneasy. "Are we spending the night on the boat? It's not exactly what I had in mind for my wedding night."

"Nope."

I stopped near the end of the docks where larger boats were kept, smiling as I saw what Bentley had arranged. Small lanterns lit up the wood planks all the way to the end, where, moored and floating in the harbor was a large, beautiful houseboat, aptly named, *New Beginnings.*

I turned to Jordan, who was staring at the boat with undisguised lust. I waved my hand. "Ta-da!"

He blinked, then looked at me. "You arranged a night for us on this boat?" he asked.

I shook my head. "I arranged the next two weeks on this boat, Jordan."

He gaped at me, speechless. I pulled him down the dock and onto the boat. Inside, he stared, his gaze bouncing from the comfortable cabin, the well-equipped galley, the outside seating area, and down the hall to the sleeping quarters.

"I don't understand."

I stepped in front of him. "You told me once you dreamed of taking one of these boats and touring the Thousand Islands. I told Bentley and asked him for help in chartering one. He became so interested, the company bought one. They did some work on it, and we get it for the next two weeks for our honeymoon."

"You did this for me?"

"Yes. Hiding it from you was hard, but Bentley and Van covered well."

"They did. I never suspected or heard anything."

"I wanted to give you—give us—this." I cupped his cheeks. "Two weeks of the open water, relaxing in the sun, and time together."

"Sandy," he whispered, then clasped me in his arms, laughing and crying at the same time. "This is amazing, my darling. Simply amazing."

He kissed me hard, lifting me off my feet. "I should have carried you over the threshold."

I smiled against his mouth, kissing him again before he set me back on my feet. I eased back before he could distract me. I indicated the pile of documents. "Those are all the maps and courses. There will be someone here in the morning to show you how it all works and answer any questions." I smiled. "Bentley offered to get someone to drive it, but I said no. I wanted to be alone with you."

He moved to the counter, looking over the papers. "Good. I have manned one before. I went with a group of men on an excursion a few years ago. They travel slowly so you have a chance to enjoy your surroundings. As long as I have the maps and chart our course, I'm good. I'll know where we can dock, and we can decide what stops we want along the way."

He looked up from the charts, his eyes filled with excitement. "I think this is the best present I have ever gotten, Sandy. Thank you." He held out his hand. "The best part is I get to share it with you."

I let him draw me to his side. I nestled against him as he slowly flipped the pages, tracing paths with his finger, tapping various spots. "So much to choose from."

"Bentley assures me if you enjoy it, we can have it again, Jordan. We don't have to see it all on one trip."

He abandoned the maps and wrapped me in his arms. "I'm looking forward to seeing everything with you, Sandy. Lots of boat trips, new cities, galleries, and places to explore. I want us to live every moment together and enjoy whatever life has to offer."

"I like the sound of that."

He bent, nuzzling my lips. "I think our course can wait until the morning. Right now, there are other things I want to explore. Like what you're wearing under that sexy dress and how fast I can get you out of it."

I slid my arms around his neck. "I like that idea."

I gasped as he swung me into his arms. "Then let's go and explore, my darling wife.

EIGHT YEARS LATER

I woke, blinking in the early morning. The sun wasn't even up yet, the only sounds outside the gentle waves breaking on the shore and, much closer to my ear, Jordan's deep, steady breathing. His arm was thrown over me, and he was a wall of warmth against my back, keeping me safe, even in his sleep.

I eased out from under his arm, sliding my feet into my slippers and grabbing the leggings and long shirt I had left at the end of the bed. I slipped into the bathroom, quietly dressed and got ready, then headed for the kitchen. I switched on the coffeepot, overriding the timer I had set for later. I couldn't wait that long.

Once it was ready, I headed outside and walked to the beach to watch the day begin.

I settled in the lounger, drawing my legs to my chest as the dawn broke. Thousands of shards of light scattered across the water, reflecting like diamonds in the early morning sun. The gulls soared high, swooped and dipped in their graceful flight, and I knew the rest of the world would soon wake. I loved coming out here in the mornings, enjoying the peacefulness of the place. Most evenings, Jordan and I sat on the back deck watching the sunset together, but the mornings were usually mine alone.

BAM never did develop the resort Bentley had planned for Port Albany. More than once, he had approved plans, only to stop construction before it started. Aiden and Cami's house sat alone on the beautiful land, with no neighbors. Bentley didn't even commence building his own planned cottage.

Finally, Aiden and Maddox met with him, asking his reasoning. I sat in on the meeting at their request. Aiden was worried that Bentley would sell off the land, and he wanted to purchase some of it to ensure their privacy if that was the case. Bentley surprised us all when he hesitated, drumming on the desk with his fingers, tugging on his sleeves—all nervous tells for Bentley, who usually displayed no nerves at all.

"I don't want to sell or develop it. At least, not to outside interests."

"What do you want to do with it?" Aiden asked after exchanging a glance with Maddox.

Bentley was silent, then he met my eyes. I saw something in his expression. It was wary and unsure—very unlike Bentley.

177

"Just tell us," I encouraged, wondering at his reticence.

"I want to keep it. Build houses for us."

For a moment, there was silence.

"Us?" Maddox questioned.

"Well, anyone interested," Bentley amended.

"I'm confused," Aiden admitted.

Bentley leaned back. "I was talking to Richard one day while he was here. The night we were at your place for dinner, Aiden. We were on the deck, looking at the water. He wondered why I had never gone ahead with the resort idea. I told him honestly part of it was due to the fact that I didn't want you living with a resort in your backyard, Aiden. He agreed that was good planning but asked why I hadn't divided the land and built some houses. Then he jokingly said I should build a BAM compound. He said he would even buy a share in a house if it was a private community." Bentley paused. "I laughed with him, but then..." His voice trailed off.

"You want to build houses for us to live in?" Maddox asked, shocked. "Bent, I'm not much for out-of-town living. You know that."

Bentley leaned forward. "What about weekends or the summer? Your kids love going to see Aiden. So do mine. What if we had a place to stay for a night or two—longer if we wanted?"

Aiden clapped his hands. "That is an awesome idea."

Bentley looked my way. "Any chance you and Jordan would like to live out that way?"

I laughed. "Jordan would love that. He'd pitch a tent there tomorrow if I told him. We've been talking about looking for a place close to the water for retirement."

They all made a face at my words, but we all knew it was going to happen at some point. Years before, I had gotten so busy that I'd hired a new assistant to help me keep up. Fee was hardworking and fit in well. She was married to Halton, and they were now part of my extended family. They had a large bunch of children, so she only worked part time these days. But she was an amazing asset to the company, and I knew she would step into my role easily. If they gave her a couple of assistants, she could work around her children's schedule and be everything the boys needed her to be. She was a natural leader, and she could handle it.

"How many houses, Bent?"

"I was thinking six. I spoke with Richard the other day and asked him if he was serious. He said he was if he could share since they would only be able to come in the summers and the occasional holiday now Gracie is in school. But he loved the idea."

"I should talk to him about shared ownership," Maddox mused. "That might work out well for us both."

"Maybe a semi-detached. You each have half."

"That would work."

I smiled to myself. Bentley, Aiden, and Maddox were close. But Bentley and Aiden had a special bond. I knew Maddox had always felt a bit outside their friendship, but since meeting Richard, he had formed his own bond there. It was good to see.

"How would you design it?"

Bentley sat up, excited. "The way the land sits, it's perfect. Almost a ring of houses, one set higher than the other, but all with views of the water. The center would be a common area."

Maddox nodded. "And BAM keeps the land, right? Same as Aiden? He owns the house, but the land is leased."

"Yes, a lifetime lease with the option for his children to re-lease for another ninety-nine years. And so on until BAM ceases to exist, then the land goes up for sale."

"And the houses?"

"If you want it built, BAM designs it, with your input. They'll have the same feel but not the same look. Each one will be individual."

"I count four in this room," Aiden said.

"Plus Reid. You know he'll want in," Maddox stated.

"Five."

"Van and Halton would probably share. Maybe another semi," Aiden mused. "If designed right, it would look really cool."

I laughed, and three sets of eyes looked at me.

"Sandy?" Bentley asked.

"A BAM compound. Only you, Bentley."

He chuckled, then became serious. "I can't imagine sharing that spot with anyone else. It stirred something inside me the day we looked at it. Emmy *finally made me realize the reason I keep backing out of starting to build is I don't want anyone else to live there but us."*

Aiden jumped up. *"Let's do this. BAM!"*

A couple of years later, Jordan and I sold the condo and moved here. We loved the house—the peacefulness of the area, the light-filled rooms, and having the boys and their kids around so much. The added bonus for Jordan was his boat that was parked right at the end of the long dock. He often took the boat out for a sail on sunny days, and I knew he looked forward to more time on the water.

We had all the privacy we wanted, but the center of the "circle of life," as Aiden dubbed it, was constantly busy. There were a couple of fire pits, a large pool, swings, and plenty of places to sit and enjoy. The three front houses, the largest buildings, had direct access to the beach. Aiden was on one end, Bentley on the other, and Jordan and I between them. Behind us, Maddox and Richard shared a place on the other side of Aiden's, Reid was in the middle, and Van and Halton split the last house. The houses were all staggered so they could see the water. In the summer months and holidays, our little grouping was bursting. Other times, it was Aiden, his family, and us. I loved it all the time.

Today, however, was a special day. It was my husband's birthday, and he was retiring. I had a huge day of celebrations planned, and everyone would be here. Richard and his family had flown in yesterday. Gina, Eric, and their children would arrive later this morning, Warren travelling with them. Colin was coming out with Miranda, his wife now for almost six years. They had two children, and we saw them often. Sadly, Jennifer wasn't able to come from Europe, but she sent Jordan a gift he would open later. Aaron came to see us last week while he was in town, still as busy as ever and unable to attend today since he would be out of the country on business.

I startled at movement out of the corner of my eye. Jordan stood, holding two mugs of coffee. "Room for one more on there?"

I smiled and shifted forward on the lounger. He slipped in behind me, handing me a mug. "I saw you down here and figured you'd need a refill." He slid his arm around my waist, tucking me tight to his chest, dropping a kiss to my head. "Hello, my darling," he murmured against my hair.

I leaned my head on his shoulder, peeking up at him. "Hello, my love."

"You're up earlier than usual. Today have you in knots?"

I laughed. "Today is simply a day of joy. I have caterers coming who will look after the meals. The tent is already set up in the circle. The band will be here for music and dancing later. Our family will be here—all of them," I added drolly.

His chest rumbled in amusement. "All hundred of them."

"It feels like it some days."

Bentley and Emmy had three children and Aiden five, thanks to the surprise addition of triplets from Cami's last pregnancy. She made him get a vasectomy after that. Maddox and Dee had two. Reid and Becca had two, but Becca was pregnant with their third. Van and Liv had their three, and Halton—the man who swore he would never have children—had four, and Fee was heavily pregnant with number five. Richard had the same number—five little VanRyans running around, driving him crazy. Or so he said. Watching the way he played with them, his patience never giving out, was an amazing thing to witness. Both he and Halton were natural fathers, and it warmed my heart, seeing them with their children. Add in Colin's two, Gina and Eric's three, and the compound would be bursting with everyone today. I was Nan to all of them, and Jordan was Pops. We loved our titles and the craziness that happened when any of them was around. Hugs, kisses, playtime—all of it. They loved spending time on the boat with Jordan, cooking in the kitchen with me, walking with us on the beach. We loved every moment.

We'd also invited some friends—many of whom we met at the dancing club and through our boating adventures. I planned it so the daytime was filled with family-friendly events, and once dinner was over, I had hired enough caregivers so the parents could relax and enjoy a night of dancing and fun while the kids happily slumbered in their beds.

It promised to be a great day. I wanted to celebrate Jordan's birthday and retirement with those he loved the most. Our twenty-six-plus grandkids and great-grandkids ranked highest for him. He thought of Colin and Jennifer as his as well, despite their being grown-ups, the same way I felt about his kids. He and Aaron got along very well, even making a few fishing trips together. We were truly a blended family, but somehow, it all worked for us.

"Thank you for today." Jordan murmured. "It's going to be wonderful."

I patted his hand.

"Have you told Bentley your news yet?" he asked.

"Yes. He suspected I would want to cut back once you finally retired. He wasn't shocked."

"I bet he wasn't happy either."

"Fee will still be there part time. He was so worried about her leaving to be at home with her kids, he's going to let her hire two other assistants so they can all job share. I suspect Agatha is going to be the star—she's a natural, and the boys like her. On any given day, there will be three people to look after them. They'll manage."

Jordan chuckled. "Three people to cover you stepping back to three days a week."

"Two days a week."

Jordan sat up, twisting me around. "Two?"

"Happy birthday. You said you wanted more time with me. You got it. I'm going in on Mondays and Thursdays. The rest of the time, I'm yours."

He kissed me, tasting like coffee and mint and Jordan. "Best gift ever."

I chuckled. "Let's see if you think that when I'm ordering you around."

He leaned back, sipping his coffee. "I like you bossing me around."

"Uh-huh."

We were quiet, listening to the sound of the water.

"I suppose I should go get ready. I have a lot of organizing to do," I murmured, loathe to move.

"Stay one more minute."

"All right."

He tightened his arm around me. "Thank you, Sandy, for today. For loving me. For giving me this beautiful, crazy, outrageously large family to be part of." He drew in a slow breath. "When Anna died, I wasn't sure I would ever really live again. Our life together has been so much more than I ever expected."

I turned and looked at him. "You gave me my life back as well."

"It's been amazing."

"We still have years ahead of us."

He leaned forward and kissed me. "I look forward to them all."

Fireworks exploded, brilliant flashes of light streaking across the sky. Rockets spread thousands of stars in the dark, twisting rivers of diamonds floating through the air, disappearing into the water. The children who were still awake cheered. For those who fell asleep, there would be an earlier display for them to look forward to tomorrow that the boys would take care of. All around us, the adults oohed and aahed, enjoying the spectacle. Jordan held me close, his breath warm on my neck as he rested his head beside mine. He brushed his lips over my neck, making me shiver, silently conveying a promise of more later. It was a promise I looked forward to him keeping.

The day had been a success. The afternoon had been spent with all the children and the families gathered in the circle. There were games and a barbecue, lots of laughter and teasing. Aiden tackled Maddox into the swimming pool, then Richard jumped in to help Maddox attempt to drown Aiden, and soon the pool was full of adults and kids alike, splashing, dunking and acting silly. Even Bentley got in on the action. I stood to the side, laughing at the antics, seeing Jordan in the middle of it all, enjoying himself immensely.

Dinner had been another wonderful affair, and there was music and fun until darkness descended. Then the kids went to their respective houses, while the adults danced and partied. I made sure there were lots of games and fun for the children and that their caregivers knew to let them come outside for the fireworks.

My feet were sore from dancing again, my body tired from running around all day, but seeing the happiness on Jordan's face, it was worth it. Having our large, chaotic group of family around us was perfect.

There had been one unexpected to surprise—for everyone.

We had finished dinner, and people were lingering over coffee and dessert. I watched Reid stand, cross the floor, and come to stand beside Jordan. He leaned down and spoke briefly to him. Jordan listened, smiled widely, and nodded.

Reid straightened and moved the center of the room, holding a glass of wine in his hand. He stuck two fingers in his mouth and whistled, getting everyone's attention.

"What is he doing?" I leaned over and asked Jordan. "We aren't doing speeches. You said you didn't want to."

"An addition," he replied. "An excellent one."

I looked over at Bentley, who seemed as confused as I was. Then I focused my attention on Reid. He had changed in the past years, growing and maturing. No longer relying on T-shirts and jeans to hide behind, he had become comfortable in his own skin. He wore suits and ties, carried himself taller. He was confident and well-spoken now. Respected by his peers and fellow staff members. He was protective of his wife and children and was an amazing father—family came first for him. Both his own, and the BAM one.

He cleared his throat. "Can everyone hear me?"

There was a return of yeses, and he smiled.

"I know today is all about Jordan. His birthday and retirement—on which I congratulate him for both."

After the smattering of applause, he smiled. "With Jordan's permission, I'm going to point the spotlight on to someone else for a moment. Our gracious hostess, Sandy."

I startled and began to protest, but Jordan caught my eye and shook his head.

"Most of you know my story. Many of you don't. I won't bore you with it,

except to say my childhood wasn't good. I made some mistakes as a teenager and ended up in jail."

There were some murmurs in the crowd, and he lifted his shoulder. "I was an idiot and made bad choices."

He turned in my direction. "After I got out, I needed a job. I saw an ad for the IT department and showed up unannounced at the BAM offices, resume in hand." He paused. "The first person I spoke to was Sandy."

"Hey, I was there!" Aiden protested.

Reid grinned. "Yes, you were. But it was Sandy who convinced you to give me an interview."

Aiden laughed. "Truth."

"Anyway, Sandy, for some reason, saw something in me. When I started working there, she took me under her wing and cared for me. She became my friend, coworker, and so much more." His voice caught. "She became the mother I never had. In fact, I would go so far as to say, if it weren't for her, I wouldn't be here today."

I felt the tears gather in my eyes. Jordan slipped his hand over mine and squeezed.

"Sandy is all about tough love. She tells it like it is, but her honesty is always laced with kindness. She is caring, warm, and I truly adore her. I am grateful—we at BAM are all grateful—to have her in our lives. She is the glue that holds us together."

He paused, clearing his throat. "She has been with me for every step of my journey, and as she and Jordan begin this next step in theirs, I wanted to tell her I'm ready to return the favor." He met my watery gaze. "I support you in anything you do, one hundred percent."

"Unless it's not working at all," Aiden shouted out.

I laughed at his announcement.

Reid nodded sagely. "Unless it's that. You get her part of the time, but not all yet, Jordan."

"Got it!" Jordan retorted.

"Sandy gave me some good advice once. She told me to grab life. Live it. I'm thrilled to see her taking her own advice and running with it." He studied me for a brief moment.

"I think Sandy is special to each person here tonight. Adoptive mom to *many, Nan to—" he waved his hand "—hundreds, friend, co-worker, and of course, beloved wife of the star of the show, Jordan."*

Jordan did a catcall. "Sandy is always the star."

"Which is why, my friend, we are here today. I know you think it's for you, but really, we're all here for Sandy."

"I knew it," Jordan responded, winking at me.

Amid the laughter, I wiped my eyes.

"So, before we get to dancing and celebrating Jordan again, I would like to raise my glass and propose a toast." He lifted his glass, waiting until everyone joined him.

"To Sandy, our hostess. Our mother, and our friend. Thank you for everything. As usual, you have outdone yourself."

I could barely swallow my sip.

Reid huffed out a sigh. "I will let you get on with your evening. Thank you."

Applause rang out, and I stood. When Reid approached, I wrapped my arms around him, holding him tight.

"That was not part of the program," I chided gently.

"You're allowed one mistake. You deserve a little spotlight."

I cupped his cheek. "I love you, my boy."

Despite the glimmer of tears in his eyes, he smiled. "I know. I'm your favorite."

I winked and he chuckled, enveloping me in his arms once again. "I love you, Sandy."

A large bang brought me out of my musings, and I glanced up at the sky as the trail of brilliance erupted. Feeling the emotion of earlier hit me again, I wiped away a tear. I met Bentley's gaze, and he smiled knowingly at me. He had been as surprised as me at Reid's impromptu toast, but he was pleased.

"Our boy has grown up, Sandy," he murmured as we danced.

As usual, away from the office, his demeanor was warm and relaxed. He was charming and witty, at ease with himself. He loved spending time with his Emmy and their children. They were his entire world. Emmy stood in front of him, and his arms held her close. She was so small, she fit under his chin, and he had to lean down to rest his chin on her head. I loved watching them together.

Beside him stood Aiden, his right-hand and best friend. Tall and broad, he towered over everyone. He had Cami tucked to his side, the protector of his family. The protector for all of those he loved. He now lived life to the fullest, shying away from nothing. Especially his feelings. He was open and passionate.

Maddox laughed, the fireworks reflecting on the lenses of his glasses. Dee smiled up at him and he lowered his face to hers to kiss her, showing his love for her freely. He had come so far from the man who refused to admit love could even be a possibility for him.

Richard VanRyan was next to him—Maddox's closest confidant and friend to all at BAM. He was such an integral part of our lives, I couldn't imagine an event without him. Loyal and steadfast, he belonged to our group. His wife, Katy, was nestled in his embrace, the rock in his world. They were an amazing couple.

Reid stood close to me, as he always did at any event. His words still echoed in my head, making me smile. Becca sat in a chair, not wanting to miss the fireworks but too tired to stand. He was behind her, his hands on her shoulders, keeping her close. The boy who had made my heart ache for his loneliness had grown into a caring, wonderful husband. He smiled when I caught his eye, silently asking if I was okay. He had been a little worried I would be upset over his toast, but there was no way I could be anything but deeply touched. He wore his heart on his sleeve, and I was proud to be one of those that he loved.

Van stood to the side, Mila on his shoulders, carefully held in place with one of his large hands. Sammy and Liv were tucked beside him. Reed stood in front of him, Van's other hand resting on his shoulder. Reed would get excited and point something out to Van, who would smile and ruffle his hair or squeeze his shoulder. Van was the gentle giant who loved hard, especially when it came to his family.

Halton was a late addition to our blended family but loved. Aloof and cool when I had first met him, he had changed and found himself, thanks to Fee and the love she brought out in him. He wasn't with us on the beach, but I knew he was on the deck at his house, sitting with Fee, and no doubt surrounded by his children. The loner, no longer alone, and complete only when with his family.

How far they had all come.

All my boys were settled, happy. They were the tapestry of my life, woven in bright, beautiful colors that lit my world. Because of them, I had a life I loved. Because of their dream, I'd had something to live for after I lost Max. Because of BAM, I found Jordan and discovered a new life. Not better, but different—just the way Jordan had said. They were all my family—loved through the heart or brought into my life through marriage, they were mine. All of them.

As if sensing my growing emotion, Jordan tucked me tight to his side, pressing a kiss to my head.

"This has been one of the best days ever, my darling. Thank you."

He was right. I was surrounded by love.

And all of this happened because three lonely young men met in college and became friends. Together, they formed their own family and built an empire.

I would never forget meeting them that fateful day as they argued over household chores in their backyard. Their lack of knowledge about how to do anything was obvious, and it brought out my maternal instincts. I had stepped in to give them a hand and soon found myself immersed in their world.

They added a depth to my life I had been missing, and somehow, I gave them what they needed. I became the love they could accept, until they were able to love themselves enough to find the person they were meant to share their life with. And because of their love, I was strong enough to do the same when it was my time to find love again.

They were the sons I never had, the businessmen I was honored to be associated with, and they had all become the men I knew they would be one day.

But they were, and always would be, boys to me.

The BAM boys.

My boys.

Thank you so much for reading SANDY - VESTED INTEREST BOOK 7. If you are so inclined, reviews are always welcome by me at your eretailer.

I rarely cry when writing-and I am not sure I have ever wept while editing. I did-twice. And when I reached the words at the bottom of the page and realized my BAM series was done-I was snotty mess.

If you have not met the VanRyan clan, Richard and Katy VanRyan's story begins with my series The Contract. You meet a more arrogant version of Richard, which makes his story much sweeter when he falls.

If you love a hero who is looking for a new beginning, Linc, from my novel The Summer of Us, would be a recommended standalone to read next. It is a story of second chances set in the small-town of Mission Cove.

If you'd like another glimpse into the Vested Interest family's future, click below to grab a little more time with them - Extended Epilogue Sandy available at Bookfunnel: https://BookHip.com/HSCPNX

Enjoy reading! Melanie

ACKNOWLEDGMENTS

As always, I have some people to thank. The ones behind the words that encourage and support. The people who make my books possible for so many reasons.

Lisa, thank you for all you do. You deserve all the wine.

Beth, Trina, Melissa, Peggy, and Deb—thank you for your feedback and support.
You gift me with your time and care and I thank you for that.

Karen, what started as a simple email had become one of the most important, treasured relationships in my life.
Thank you for holding my hand, laughing at my incompetence,
drying my tears,
and making me laugh.
You are a star. *My* star. (ahem)

To all the bloggers, readers, and especially my promo team. Thank you for everything you do. Shouting your love of books—of my work, posting, sharing—your recommendations keep my TBR list full, and the support you have shown me is deeply appreciated.

To my fellow authors who have shown me such kindness, thank you. I will follow your example and pay it forward.

My reader group, Melanie's Minions—love you all.

And my Matthew—all my love—always.

MY BOOKS

Vested Interest Series

BAM - The Beginning (Prequel)

Bentley (Vested Interest #1)

Aiden (Vested Interest #2)

Maddox (Vested Interest #3)

Reid (Vested Interest #4)

Van (Vested Interest #5)

Halton (Vested Interest #6)

Sandy (Vested Interest #7)

Insta-Spark Collection

It Started with a Kiss

Christmas Sugar

An Instant Connection

An Unexpected Gift

The Contract Series

The Contract (The Contract #1)

The Baby Clause (The Contract #2)

The Amendment (The Contract #3)

Mission Cove

The Summer of Us

Standalones

Into the Storm

Beneath the Scars

Over the Fence

My Image of You (Random House/Loveswept)

Revved to the Maxx

ABOUT THE AUTHOR

NYT/WSJ/USAT international bestselling author Melanie Moreland, lives a happy and content life in a quiet area of Ontario with her beloved husband of thirty-plus years and their rescue cat, Amber. Nothing means more to her than her friends and family, and she cherishes every moment spent with them.

While seriously addicted to coffee, and highly challenged with all things computer-related and technical, she relishes baking, cooking, and trying new recipes for people to sample. She loves to throw dinner parties, and enjoys traveling, here and abroad, but finds coming home is always the best part of any trip.

Melanie loves stories, especially paired with a good wine, and enjoys skydiving (free falling over a fleck of dust) extreme snowboarding (falling down stairs) and piloting her own helicopter (tripping over her own feet.) She's learned happily ever afters, even bumpy ones, are all in how you tell the story.

Melanie is represented by Flavia Viotti at Bookcase Literary Agency. For any questions regarding subsidiary or translation rights please contact her at flavia@bookcaseagency.com

Connect with Melanie

Like reader groups? Lots of fun and giveaways! Check it out Melanie Moreland's Minions
Join my newsletter for up-to-date news, sales, book announce-

ments and excerpts (no spam). Click here to sign up Melanie Moreland's newsletter

or visit https://www.subscribepage.com/melaniemoreland

Visit my website www.melaniemoreland.com

facebook.com/authormoreland

twitter.com/morelandmelanie

instagram.com/morelandmelanie

Made in the USA
Middletown, DE
22 June 2020